D1200841

"Only a very few in the ecumenical movement today are as qualified as Michael Kinnamon to take on some of the thorny questions that plague the movement in our day, and only a few have the knowledge, commitment, and courage to discuss them the way Kinnamon does in this volume.... A must-read for those concerned about the future of the ecumenical movement."

— S. WESLEY ARIARAJAH
Drew University

"Insightful, direct, and greatly invested in the ecumenical movement, Kinnamon helps us traverse the changing ecumenical landscape with concrete steps and a positive, realistic global perspective. *Can a Renewal Movement Be Renewed?* is a must-read for all who care and want to do something about the revitalization that the church so desperately needs."

— MARILYN MECHAM
*former president of Ecumenical and
Interreligious Leaders Network*

"This book gives us a glimpse into the mind and heart of someone who has earned his place as a valued leader among America's diverse church traditions. It reveals Michael Kinnamon as both teacher and student, as having profound wisdom, humility, and magnanimity — qualities that can guide whole churches into a deeper engagement with each other and into a more dynamic engagement with the world."

— ARCHBISHOP VICKEN AYKAZIAN
*Armenian Orthodox Church
Christian Churches Together*

Can a Renewal Movement Be Renewed?

Questions for the Future of Ecumenism

Michael Kinnamon

WILLIAM B. EERDMANS PUBLISHING COMPANY
GRAND RAPIDS, MICHIGAN / CAMBRIDGE, U.K.

Published 2014 by
Wm. B. Eerdmans Publishing Co.
2140 Oak Industrial Drive N.E., Grand Rapids, Michigan 49505 /
P.O. Box 163, Cambridge CB3 9PU U.K.
www.eerdmans.com

Printed in the United States of America

20 19 18 17 16 15 14   7 6 5 4 3 2 1

Library of Congress Cataloging-in-Publication Data

Kinnamon, Michael.
    Can a renewal movement be renewed?: questions for the future of ecumenism /
    Michael Kinnamon.
        pages   cm
    Includes bibliographical references and index.
    ISBN 978-0-8028-7075-9 (pbk.: alk. paper)
    1. Ecumenical movement — Miscellanea.
    2. Christian Union — Miscellanea.   I. Title.
    BX8.3.K49   2014
    262.001'1 — dc23

                               2013043135

For Mardine, wonderful partner in dialogue and in life

Contents

CHAPTER 1

Does Ecumenism Have a Future?

There is no doubt that ecumenism occupies a prominent place in the history of the church in the twentieth century. "The ecumenical movement," writes the British theologian Paul Avis,

> has not simply replaced suspicion, incomprehension and rivalry with understanding, trust and friendship — though in itself that is no mean achievement. In the form of theological dialogue, ecumenism has also significantly scaled down the extent of church-dividing issues between Christian traditions . . . [and] has established that there is "a certain, albeit imperfect, communion" between churches that are not yet in full communion.[1]

In the form of councils of churches, the movement has enabled previously competing denominations to pray for and with one another; to bear common witness to Jesus Christ, instead of only recruiting for "our brand" of Christianity; to join in concerted action against racism, war, and economic oppression; and to engage in shared service on behalf of those in need.

Even where a closer structured relationship has proved difficult, churches have changed through encounter with Christian sisters and brothers in other confessions and cultures. To say it another way, churches have

---

1. Paul Avis, "Unreal Worlds Meeting," an unpublished paper presented at a conference, "Where We Dwell in Common: Pathways for Dialogue in the 21st Century," held in Assisi, Italy, in April 2012.

been *renewed* through mutual sharing of the gifts each has received thanks to their distinctive experiences of God's presence and power. Worship has been enriched. Understandings of mission have expanded. Communities have become more inclusive. Such renewal is by no means incidental to the goal of ecumenism, since the unity envisioned in the ecumenical movement has never been simply a mutual acceptance of what we now are, but, rather, a "common quest for the renewed obedience of the one church of Jesus Christ in its faith, its life, its mission, and its compassionate response to the world's anguish."[2] Ecumenism has been a movement for unity through renewal and of renewal through unity.[3]

It is not clear, however, that this ecumenical impulse, at least in its past forms, will figure prominently in the church of the twenty-first century. While some full communion agreements have been officially adopted in recent years, they don't (yet) make much of a difference in the life of most members in the pews; and much theology produced through inter-church dialogue seems destined to gather dust rather than promote renewal. Meanwhile, councils of churches from local to global struggle to keep the doors open in the face of reduced funding — which, of course, limits their creativity and impact. *New York Times* columnist Ross Douthat speaks for many outside observers when he writes that the ecumenical movement has borne real theological fruit, "but what began as a daring experiment has decayed into bureaucratized complacency — a dull round of interdenominational statements . . . only tenuously connected to the gospel."[4]

And so the question that is the title of this book: Can a renewal movement be renewed? Can the ecumenical movement, which gave such energy and direction to the church in the twentieth century, be reconceived in

2. David M. Gill, "Whom God Hath Joined Together: Churches and Councils of Churches," *Ecumenical Review* 42 (January 1991): 46. This theme of renewal as central to ecumenism is explored more extensively in my book *The Vision of the Ecumenical Movement and How It Has Been Impoverished by Its Friends* (St. Louis: Chalice Press, 2003), pp. 23-35.

3. I have colleagues who think "ecumenism" should not be in the title of this book because it will limit the book's appeal. "In an interfaith age," they contend, "ecumenism is old hat. And, besides, it carries lots of negative baggage for some Christians." Well, maybe. But I continue to use the term because I know of no alternative to the complex of meanings it evokes. "Christian unity" captures it in part; but that alone doesn't point to the multiple "streams" — justice, education, mission, service, dialogue — of this movement. Nor does it suggest how renewal is inseparable from unity in the vision so often articulated by ecumenical leaders over the past one hundred years.

4. Ross Douthat, "Benedict's Gambit," *The New York Times* (October 25, 2009), accessible at http://www.nytimes.com/2009/10/26/opinion/26douthat.html?emc=eta1.

a way that provides renewing power for the church in this era? I believe that the answer to this question is a qualified "yes" (with the help of God), and the chapters that follow are, in part, an attempt to say how this might happen.

Exploring the Question

This book is not a blueprint for the full renewal that is needed, but, I hope, a contribution to it. I realize that I am too invested in the current movement, perhaps too appreciative of the gains made, to grasp fully the new things God is doing in our midst. I am also aware of the tensions inherent in any single prescription for renewal. Can the revolution in communications technology bring new vitality to ecumenism? Yes, surely. But the key discipline of the ecumenical movement has been face-to-face dialogue and relationship building, and I cannot help but lament anything that undermines it. Can new evangelical and Pentecostal partners give fresh energy to the movement? Yes, surely. But ecumenical leaders have rightly insisted that unity is inseparable from social justice, and I know that expanding the table often reduces the range of justice commitments the churches can make together. Can the leadership of young adults lead to new ways of thinking and acting ecumenically? Yes, surely. But I am convinced that an orientation to the future must not forget the achievements of the past, lest we spend time reinventing rather than building on what has already been accomplished. Can the growing focus on interfaith relations expand the search for human wholeness that is central to the ecumenical vision? Yes, surely. But the ecumenical movement has been grounded in the conviction that in Christ we have seen God's most decisive work of reconciling love — that the church, the community of Christ's followers, is called to be a sign of such reconciliation — and I pray we will never back away from this witness.

This book, then, is an effort to name the problems, identify strengths and accomplishments on which we can build, and suggest steps that can move us in the direction of revitalization, especially at the local level. What those who care about ecumenism can now least afford is business as usual. Over the past two generations, what began as a passionate, even revolutionary, effort to reverse centuries of division and fragmentation has become a taken-for-granted part of the churches' structure (an office of "external relations"), often now manifest in organizations to which the churches belong rather than an integral part of who we are. The luster of novelty has worn off, and many Christians no longer are moved by the astonishing privilege of being with those who are different.

The chapters that follow were originally speeches — for the most part, ones that I delivered while serving as general secretary of the National Council of Churches, 2008 to 2011. While they have all been substantially rewritten for inclusion in this volume — removing specific references, eliminating areas of duplication — I have tried to retain some of the fast-paced tempo of a speech. These presentations were generally made to audiences that included persons well versed in ecumenism as well as those for whom this is new territory. It is my hope that these chapters will appeal to the same range of readers — addressing questions of interest to old hands and students of the movement (reviewing history, summarizing developments), but not getting so deep in the weeds of ecumenical debates that other readers lose interest.

The chapters vary a good deal in style and format (one chapter is even in the form of an "open letter"); but, taken as a whole, the book is intended to be

- very practical, offering concrete steps for living ecumenically (there are lots of lists!);
- global in perspective yet oriented toward local action;
- attentive to the history of the ecumenical movement, but also focused on implications for the present and future;
- particularly concerned with difficult issues and tensions that face the churches;
- both upbeat about what has been accomplished over the past one hundred years and realistic about the challenges before us.

The fifteen chapters cover a variety of topics, but this is by no means a comprehensive treatment of ecumenism. If that were the intent, there would need to be chapters specifically on such topics as mission, young adults, education, the use of the Bible, and, especially, prayer and worship — which I, like Pope John Paul II, regard as the heart of the ecumenical impulse. If this renewal movement is to be renewed, then we must not reduce a divine initiative to a purely human enterprise!

Why Ecumenism?

I have devoted much of my ministry to the work of ecumenism — as a staff member of the World Council of Churches' (WCC) Faith and Order

Commission, as general secretary of the Consultation on Church Union, as general secretary of the National Council of Churches, and as a professor of ecumenical and interfaith studies for more than twenty-five years. Why? Because, like many others, I long for a church better than the one I see around us. I stand in awe of the faithfulness of many Christians. The way they hold together firm commitment to Christ with active acceptance of others is humbling and inspiring. But the picture presented by the corporate church is often quite different: co-opted by the culture, intolerant of those who are different, tepid in its social witness, and, despite decades of dialogue, still fragmented into competing factions engaged in a predatory scramble for new members. The ecumenical movement was never the answer to all of these problems, but it has been and, I believe, can still be the context within which churches experience the renewal they so desperately need.

I am also invested in this movement because — contrary to what we often hear — the world is so ready for it! In an age of terrorism, when many persons are increasingly afraid of those who are different, the ecumenical church can demonstrate what it means to welcome the stranger. In a political climate marked by ideological polarization, the ecumenical church can provide a model for staying at the table in the face of real disagreement. In an era when diversity is exalted and unity viewed with suspicion, the ecumenical church can show why the two belong together. In a society where justice is generally pursued in like-minded groups, the ecumenical church can be an example of how unity and justice are inseparable. These claims are explored and defended from different angles in the chapters that follow.

In a presentation to the WCC's Central Committee in 1973, the ecumenical leader Lukas Vischer posed an intriguing question: How will these present times strike our ecumenical descendants when they look back on them several decades from now? What will future generations make of all our strenuous efforts to give visible expression to the church's unity? "Perhaps," writes Vischer, "our successors will smile and say: 'What curious people they must have been in those days. . . . Should it not have been obvious to them, even then, that they were doomed to failure from the start?' . . . Or will they say: 'What strange problems they were still wrestling with in those days!'" Why did it seem so difficult to recognize that we are, in fact, one church?[5]

The forty years since Vischer's question have been chastening. Whatever made us think that the Roman Catholic Church would soon join the WCC

---

5. Lukas Vischer, "A Report to the Central Committee," *Ecumenical Review* 25 (October 1973): 482-83.

or that united churches, such as the United Church of Christ or the Church of South India, would continue to proliferate around the world? Whatever made us believe that fear of change wouldn't compromise the results of rational theological dialogue? Whatever made us think that the excitement of early ecumenical encounters wouldn't dissipate once the demands of unity set in?

A better question, we now realize, may be this: Can the ecumenical movement continue to be a vital and relevant framework as the churches grope their way toward deeper engagement? Can this renewal movement be renewed?

CHAPTER 2

What Would It Mean to Take the "Next Step" in Ecumenical and Interfaith Relations?

It often seems, here in the second decade of the twenty-first century, that the ecumenical and interfaith movements are stuck in the status quo. During the last half of the twentieth century, relations between many churches clearly improved. For much of that time, ecumenism was fresh and exciting — the "great new fact of our era," as William Temple called it — and there was a feeling that the ecumenical movement was truly moving. At the same time, dialogue and cooperation between various religious communities, especially Christians and Jews, took dramatic steps forward.

In recent years, however, the momentum has definitely slowed. Ecumenical relations seem to have reached a plateau; and even interfaith work, the great new fact of *this* era, has run into imposing roadblocks. For example, many councils of churches have been reduced to cooperative agencies (whose budgets are prime targets in lean times), a status far more modest than the aspirations expressed in their defining documents. Several bilateral dialogues — for instance, that between the Episcopal Church and the Evangelical Lutheran Church in America — have reached substantive theological agreements; but even when these result in declarations of "full communion," they seem to have made little difference, at least until now, in the way most local members live with one another. Interfaith relations have grown increasingly cordial, even cooperative; but outside events threaten the gains of recent years. For example, a half century of improved relations between Christians and Jews is in danger of being undone by differences over the Israeli-Palestinian conflict, and 9-11 certainly impacted the relationship between American Muslims and the Christian majority in this country.

Some of this was predictable. Periods of exhilarating developments are inevitably followed by times of slowed momentum as the issues get harder. To take an obvious example, the relationship between Protestants and Catholics, which gained strong tailwind from the Second Vatican Council of the 1960s, must finally come to grips with such matters as the ordination of women and the role of the papacy. I am convinced, however, that another part of the problem is that the leaders of our religious communities have trouble envisioning the "next step" in their relationships with others. Even if we can articulate long-term goals (itself a challenge), we often find it difficult to imagine what would constitute short-term progress. Such imagining is the purpose of this chapter.

A Framework for Imagination

To begin this discussion, I invite readers to envision a series of steps or stages that, for the most part, can apply to either ecumenical or interfaith relations:

> Competition — Co-existence — Cooperation —
> Commitment — Communion[1]

- *Competition* is the stage in which a church or other faith community sees itself as basically self-sufficient and in a state of rivalry with other churches or communities, which it regards as wrong in their religious claims.
- *Co-existence* is the stage in which a church, while showing little readiness for positive relations, acknowledges that Christ may be known and followed in other churches, or when a religious community agrees to live alongside others but has little interest in dialogues or structured relationships.
- *Cooperation* is the stage in which a church or other faith community recognizes others with sufficient warmth to undertake certain tasks or forms of witness together, to engage with them in real, if limited, partnership.
- *Commitment* is the stage in which simple cooperation no longer corre-

---

1. As far as I can determine, this continuum was first articulated at the assembly of the British Council of Churches in 1977. I first encountered it in a paper by Martin Conway at a consultation in 1982. The report of that meeting, including the "5 Cs," is published in *Midstream* 22 (1983): 222-37.

sponds to the degree of mutual recognition felt between the churches or faith communities, in which they affirm the existence of lasting bonds greater than expedient collaboration.

- *Communion* is the stage in which churches no longer experience themselves simply as separate entities, but, since earlier divisions have been reconciled, now try to act as one in mission and to share "sacred things." Christians generally speak of communion (the frequently used Greek term is *koinonia*) only in terms of other churches, not interfaith partners.

It is important not to claim too much for what is, after all, only a tool for spurring the imagination. For one thing, ecumenical and interfaith relationships are not as linear — progressive — as this series of stages may imply. It is certainly possible (although the stages of commitment and communion are intended to preclude it) for communities to slip backward in their relations with others. For another, all relationships are more ambiguous than any simple typology can suggest; communities may find themselves at different stages with different partners, or even with different parts of the other community. And, of course, we should never discount the possibility of breakthrough moments that disrupt old patterns of relationship and undercut any notions of "gradual growth." I have in mind the 1920 encyclical of the Holy Synod of Constantinople, sent "unto the churches of Christ everywhere," which, stunningly, called for a league or council of churches and lifted the nascent ecumenical movement to a new level of intensity.[2] Or the 1960 sermon by Eugene Carson Blake, which invited various denominations "to break through the barriers of nearly 500 years of history," an initiative that led directly to the Consultation on Church Union.[3]

Still, even with these caveats in mind, it seems important and possible to envision next steps along the way. And the "5 Cs" — competition, coexistence, cooperation, commitment, communion — provide a framework for this discussion.

2. "Unto the Churches of Christ Everywhere," in Michael Kinnamon and Brian E. Cope, eds., *The Ecumenical Movement: An Anthology of Key Texts and Voices* (Grand Rapids: Eerdmans, 1997), pp. 11-14.

3. Eugene Carson Blake, "A Proposal Toward the Reunion of Christ's Church," at http://www.churchesunitinginchrist.org/what-you-can-do/speeches/46-blake-s-sermon-pike-s-response.

Councils of Churches

Let's start with councils of churches, by which I mean not the authoritative gatherings of the ancient church (e.g., the Council of Nicea) or of some contemporary churches (e.g., the Second Vatican Council), but voluntary associations of separated churches within a given area — local, national, regional, and global. Councils of this sort developed in the course of the modern ecumenical movement and are among the movement's most widespread and widely recognized expressions.

These councils of still-divided churches were initially regarded as organizations through which denominations cooperate on matters of common concern. In recent decades, however, the official documents of councils of churches — many of them, at least — suggest a different understanding. The National Council of Churches of Christ in the USA (NCC) is a case in point. When the NCC formed in 1950, its constitution spoke of the council as "an inclusive cooperative agency" of the churches, the purpose of which was "to do for the churches such cooperative work as they authorize the council to carry out on their behalf."[4] A study of the NCC's "ecclesiological significance," produced by its Faith and Order Commission in 1963, notes dryly that "the churches when in cooperation seem to take the existing church situation somewhat for granted, and to be prepared to work cooperatively within its limits."[5]

Thirty years after the NCC formed, however, the language of its original constitution no longer seemed adequate to describe the depth of relationship that the member churches had, or aspired to, through participation in the council. Thus, in 1981, the NCC governing body adopted a new constitution that describes the council as "a community of Christian communions," which, on the basis of their shared confession of Jesus Christ, "*covenant with one another*" to manifest the unity of the church and come together in common mission.[6]

This is clearly the language of commitment, not cooperation. It is a way of saying that the essence of conciliar life is the relationship of the churches to one another, not their relationship to some external structure. The World

4. Quoted in "The Ecclesiological Significance of Councils of Churches," in Joseph A. Burgess and Jeffrey Gros, eds., *Growing Consensus: Church Dialogues in the United States, 1962-1991* (New York: Paulist Press, 1995), pp. 599-600.

5. Burgess and Gros, eds., *Growing Consensus*, p. 600.

6. See the "Preamble" to the *Constitution and Bylaws* at http://www.ncccusa.org/pdfs/ncconstitution.pdf.

Council of Churches (WCC) underlines this point in its most recent state-ment of self-definition, "Towards a Common Understanding and Vision of the WCC" (1997): "The Council *is* the fellowship of the churches on the way towards full *koinonia* [communion]. It *has* a structure and organization in order to serve as an instrument for the churches as they work towards *koinonia* in faith, life and witness; but the WCC is not to be identified with this structure. . . ."[7]

Both councils have tried to embody this new level of relationship in "Marks of Our Commitment" (NCC) or a list of actions and attitudes im-plied by membership (WCC)[8] that set forth signs of mutual accountabil-ity appropriate to a "community of Christian communions" (NCC) or a "fellowship of churches" (WCC). But I know of no one who believes that the churches have, in fact, made the move from cooperation to commit-ment within the framework of these councils. Churches, in my experience, continue to see councils as "them" rather than "us," as "that organization" rather than "our fellowship," as an association they have joined rather than a covenant they have made with others. Former WCC staff member Victor Hayward, after visiting eighty national councils of churches, put the matter this way at a 1971 consultation:

> A council committee usually means a gathering of church leaders to de-cide what the council shall do, instead of what their churches should do together through the council. The churches are not really committed to one another. . . . This means that councils are too frequently an ecumenical facade behind which the churches in practice remain as unecumenical as ever.[9]

I fear that, despite changes in constitutional language, this judgment remains generally accurate some forty years later.

What, then, would it mean in practice to move from cooperation to commitment? What, concretely, might the churches or conciliar leaders do

---

7. "Towards a Common Understanding and Vision of the WCC" (CUV), par. 3.5.2, at http://www.oikoumene.org/en/resources/documents/assembly/porto-alegre-2006/3
-preparatory-and-background-documents/common-understanding-and-vision-of-the
-WCC-CUV.html.

8. See "Marks of Our Commitment" at www.ncccusa.org/about/marks.pdf, and CUV, par. 3.7.

9. Victor Hayward, "A Survey of National Christian Councils," *International Review of Mission* 60 (1971): 518.

to help churches live out their professed desire to be a true "community of communions"? I have four recommendations:

1. *Emphasize the building of relationships among the member churches.* During my years with the NCC, we attempted to do this by visiting each member communion with a delegation made up not of staff but of representatives from other members. We worshiped together in the style of the host church, ate a meal together, exchanged gifts as a sign of our commitment to one another, and engaged in conversations around such questions as the following:

- When we (the other members) pray for you (the church being visited), for what should we pray?
- What gifts has God entrusted to you that you hope to offer within the fellowship of the council?
- What gifts do you need/hope to receive?
- What are the biggest challenges you are likely to face in the years ahead?
- What do you intend to do to strengthen your relationship with other members?

After each visit, I (the only staff on the visiting delegation) would send a letter to the head of the visited church, summarizing our discussion. I know of at least one head of communion who sent this letter to every parish, asking that it be read from the pulpit or on some suitable public occasion as a gift from that church's conciliar partners. This was, for me, a striking indication of a church that viewed its participation in the NCC in terms of commitment, not just cooperation.

2. *Promote knowledge of the other member churches within our own communion.* It is a perfectly safe bet that the vast majority of ministers — let alone, laypersons — of my own denomination, the Christian Church (Disciples of Christ), would be surprised to learn that the Disciples are part of a covenantal community that includes the Coptic Orthodox, the Korean Presbyterians, the Missionary Baptists, the Serbian Orthodox, and the Moravians. Indeed, I have had heads of communion tell me that they probably couldn't name half the NCC member churches — as if that were a badge of honor!

The "Responsibilities" associated with membership, listed in the NCC's Strategic Plan for 2007-2011, include

- Attempt to know the other members as fully as possible and to teach about them in the church's congregations and seminaries.

- Pray for the other members and for the life of the churches together in the NCC.[10]

Taking these responsibilities seriously would be an indication that the relationship has moved from cooperation to commitment.

3. *See the council as an arena for dealing with the truly divisive issues of our day.* Councils of churches, in my experience, are generally marked by what one ecumenical leader calls a "polite parallelism"[11] that avoids contentious matters, making it nearly impossible for the churches to learn from one another or to seek God's guidance together. A vital council is one where the churches dare to bring their deepest fears, passions, and concerns to the conciliar table because they affirm their given unity in Christ, even when confronted by genuine disagreement. If a church cannot ask its partners in the community of the council "What is your theological basis for ordaining persons who are gay or lesbian?" or "Why have you refrained from joining other churches in public witness for environmental protection?" where can such questions be raised? Churches at the level of cooperation avoid them for the sake of harmony. Churches at the level of commitment welcome them for the sake of mutual growth and deeper discernment of God's will.

4. *Stand with other churches in times of special need.* To take one example, the Arab Spring revolution and subsequent turmoil in Egypt may not immediately touch most churches in the NCC; but it is *the* overriding concern for the Coptic Orthodox Church. Coptic Orthodox Christians in Egypt face an uncertain future, and their anxiety is deeply felt by Coptic Orthodox in the United States. This should make the situation of Christians in Egypt a priority for *every* church in the council. If the relationship is at the level of real commitment, the other members will not wait for an invitation to stand with the Coptic Orthodox Church. They will reach out to the conciliar partner, asking how they can best be of support. And the Coptic Orthodox, in turn, will make sure that issues of concern to other members are also on their agenda.

The members of a council that has moved from cooperation to commitment will be accountable for the commitments they make to one another. Such a council will authorize the staff and elected leaders to promote accountability, perhaps by asking the churches, when gathered in assembly, to

---

10. At www.ncccusa.org/NCCdocs/NCCstrategicplan.pdf.

11. Janice Love, "From Insults to Inclusion — Common Understanding and Vision: Continuing the Discussion," *Ecumenical Review* 50 (July 1998): 376.

report on their actions. What has your church done to stimulate knowledge of, and prayer for, the others? Has your church brought its own struggles, as well as its concerns about the doctrines and practices of others, to the table for common discussion? How has your church stood by others in their time of need? Making this time of accounting a regular part of the council's assembly would not only serve as a challenge for all the members, but also offer examples of commitment to emulate.

Relationships of "Full Communion"

Communion, a translation of the Greek *koinonia,* is a term rich with biblical resonance. For Christians it generally signifies a profound intimacy with God through Christ and a concomitant intimacy with one another in Christ. Something of the meaning of the term is captured in the definition of Christian unity as a "fully committed fellowship," set forth by the WCC's New Delhi Assembly in 1961. Such a *fellowship* (another translation for *koinonia*), in the words of the assembly report, entails

> a full participation in common praise and prayer, the shared realities of penitence and forgiveness, mutuality in suffering and joy, listening together to the same gospel, responding in faith, obedience and service, joining in the one mission of Christ in the world, a self-forgetting love for all for whom Christ died, and the reconciling grace that breaks down every wall of race, colour, caste, tribe, sex, class and nation.[12]

The term "full communion" was first used to indicate the relationship between geographically separated churches which, if they were in the same place, would be one body. More recently it has been used to describe a relationship in which churches mutually recognize that the other holds the essentials of the Christian faith, recognize the validity of each other's sacraments and ordinations, and, therefore, agree to share in the sacraments and mission and to set up procedures for the interchangeability of ministry in some form. The full communion agreement between the Episcopal Church and the Evangelical Lutheran Church in America, to take a well-known example, defines the relationship as one in which "churches become inter-

12. "Report of the Section on Unity," in Kinnamon and Cope, eds., *The Ecumenical Movement,* p. 89.

dependent while remaining autonomous." In addition to the acts of mutual recognition mentioned above, these churches agree to establish "organs of regular consultation and communication" in order to "enable common witness, life, and service."[13] This is not communion as described in the New Testament or at New Delhi, but it is still a relationship of real intensity, a relationship beyond the level of commitment spoken about in connection with councils of churches.

At least in theory. In practice, it isn't clear that much has changed for local Lutherans and Episcopalians since full communion was declared in 1997. I don't mean to suggest that nothing has been accomplished. Some emergency relief efforts have been consolidated, the denominations have begun to work more closely in several chaplaincy and campus ministry settings, and a Coordinating Committee is encouraging compliance with provisions of the agreement.[14] Still, I have heard ecumenical leaders from churches with full communion agreements lament that, without real structures of mutual accountability, these relationships can become a way of feeling good about continued division; and that the conversations in national and judicatory settings are often more geared toward identifying boundaries than exploring possibilities. When the churches face internal crises, they generally still don't turn to their full communion partners or expect help from them. They speak of sharing gifts (which churches do or should do through councils), but without ensuring a way that this is taken seriously.

At best, our full communion relationships seem to express a level of commitment to one another, but not yet true communion. In my judgment, the following would be indications that the churches were actually taking the next step:

1. *Encourage and facilitate the development of covenants between local congregations.* If full communion agreements remain primarily on the national level, then they aren't "communion." Churches in each local setting should be encouraged to establish formal bonds with full communion neighbors, committing themselves to share the sacraments and mission, but also to pray for these neighbors by name and to invite their participation in the life of the community. This, of course, is happening in some places (guidelines

13. "Called to Common Mission," par. 2, at http://www.elca.org/Who-We-Are/Our -Three-Expressions/Churchwide-Organization/Office-of-the-Presiding-Bishop/Ecumenical -and-Inter-Religious-Relations/Full-Communion-Partners/The-Episcopal-Church/Called-to -Common-Mission/Official-Text.aspx.

14. See Mitzi J. Budde, "Are We There Yet?: The Task and Function of Full Communion Coordinating Committees," *Journal of Ecumenical Studies* 48 (Winter 2013).

have been developed for Lutheran-Episcopal federated and union parishes); but local covenants remain the exception, not the rule.

2. *Undertake new church development with the other wherever possible.* This is usually an area where denominationalism is on full display, as churches attempt to plant their flag on territory that holds promise for growth. Thus, doing new church starts together as a matter of course, not an exception, would truly signal a deeper level of relationship.

3. *Seek to do global mission with one another.* A central feature of the full communion relationship between the Disciples of Christ and the United Church of Christ has been the creation of a common mission board, with a single set of mission executives serving both churches.[15] I hope that this model will commend itself to other churches as an important mark of full communion. The churches may, of course, find other areas where structures or programs can be integrated (e.g., church publishing houses).

4. *Include the other fully in all planning for the future.* Churches in full communion have distinctive histories, but, in theory, a more common future. One sign of real communion is the insistence that all long-range planning be done together or, at the very least, with full communion partners at the table.

5. *Share resources when the other has need.* The implication of full communion is that, when the other is suffering financial distress or a crisis of leadership or some sort of scandal, it is happening to *us*. If the other's witness is in some way weakened, our witness is weakened. In the same way, the other church's spiritual ancestors and heroes of the faith become ours, and their strengths and successes are cause not for envy but rejoicing.

I could have mentioned, of course, the need for full implementation of the agreements already made (e.g., truly interchangeable ministry), but perhaps we can take that for granted. What I have tried to identify are other actions that would give evidence that a next step has been taken.

Jewish-Christian Relations

Interfaith relations in the West were, for centuries, primarily a matter of competition. In some parts of the world, religious communities have long co-existed; but this began to happen in the West only in the course of the past century. A prominent indication that western Christians — many of them, at

---

15. See www.globalministries.org/about-us/.

any rate — were at a new stage in their relations with people of other faiths came at the Second Vatican Council:

> The Catholic Church rejects nothing of what is true and holy in [the great world] religions. She has a high regard for the manner of life and conduct, the precepts and doctrines which, although differing in many ways from her own teaching, nevertheless often reflect a ray of that truth which enlightens all men. . . . The Church, therefore, urges her [members] to enter with prudence and charity into discussion and collaboration with members of other religions. Let Christians, while witnessing to their own faith and way of life, acknowledge, preserve and encourage the spiritual and moral truths found among non-Christians, also their social life and culture.[16]

This declaration was made in 1965. Subsequent generations have experienced a rapid growth in the religious diversity of American society and an increasing willingness to move fully into the stage of interfaith cooperation — though often with the disapproval of their co-religionists. (There is, of course, great irony in the fact that improved relations with interfaith neighbors can lead to tension, even division, within one's own community.)

This movement to cooperation has been particularly true of the relationship between Christians and Jews. In the years since World War II, with its revelation of the depths to which hatred of Jews can descend, mainline churches in the U.S. have officially, publicly repented of their complicity in such hatred, declared their opposition to all forms of anti-semitism, and affirmed God's continuing love for and covenant with the Jewish people.[17] It is now commonplace for churches and synagogues to cooperate locally, and for Jewish and Christian leaders to stand together nationally — although, as we have noted, the momentum in this relationship, so evident as recently as the 1980s, has stalled in the face of disagreements regarding the conflict in the Middle East.

The question I am asking is whether it is possible to regain momentum by envisioning a next step in the relationship, envisioning a move from co-

---

16. "Declaration on the Relation of the Church to Non-Christian Religions" *(Nostra Aetate),* in Kinnamon and Cope, eds., *The Ecumenical Movement,* p. 399.

17. See Michael Kinnamon, "Signs of Hope in Jewish/Christian Relations," in Clark M. Williamson, ed., *The Church and the Jewish People* (St. Louis: Christian Board of Publication, 1994), pp. 65-72.

operation to some form of real commitment. There are at least three things that such a move might entail:

1. A relationship of commitment would mean *going beyond trading information — beyond getting to know one another better — to a willingness to learn from one another* in ways that potentially enrich, even expand, our own faith. Christians have historically been unwilling to take this step because they see it as undermining the claims that Jesus is the definitive revelation of God and that Scripture, when taken to include what Christians call the New Testament, provides all that is necessary for salvation. Even if these claims are true, however, isn't it possible that Christians, being human, have something less than a complete grasp of God's will? Isn't it possible that the relationship others have with God may reveal new insights into God's nature and purpose, if we are open to receiving them?

Since this may be harder to envision than some other suggestions in this chapter, I want to offer a longer personal example. During my years as a professor at Eden Theological Seminary, I was privileged to co-teach a course on Jewish-Christian dialogue with Susan Talve, rabbi of Central Reform Congregation (CRC) in St. Louis. The course was marked by honest conversation on difficult issues, but none more difficult than the tension involved in what Christians call "grace and works." Rabbi Talve had generally avoided the language of "grace," because, for her, it implied human passivity in the work of redemption (the "repairing of creation"), and because it is so closely associated with Christianity. I, on the other hand, had heard "works righteousness" when moral deeds *(mitzvot)* were spoken of as religious obligations rather than responses to the graciousness of God. And I would cringe when Rabbi Talve, out of her love for Jewish mysticism, would speak of humans working to perfect the world and of "drawing God into the world" through our good deeds.

The more I listened to Rabbi Talve, however, the more I began to see (as the New Testament implies in several places) that the good news of God's gracious love for the world, while not dependent on what we do, is inseparable from our human response through acts of justice and mercy. Meanwhile, Rabbi Talve tells me, she began to realize that grace is an essential concept for a religion founded on God's initiative in fashioning creation and making covenant. As I prepared to leave St. Louis for my position at the National Council of Churches, I was invited to attend Shabbat service at CRC, where the congregation (graciously) acknowledged my teaching with their rabbi, and Susan spoke of the importance and wonder of grace.

This, it seems to me, is an example of moving beyond cooperation to commitment. Those of us involved in this extended conversation at Eden Seminary never refrained from raising difficult theological issues or compromised principles central to our faith traditions. But we did listen to one another with a hope, even an expectation, that we might learn something we hadn't learned in our own community about God and God's interaction with the world. To move from cooperation to commitment is to affirm that the other is a highly valued, perhaps even essential, partner in our own journey of faith.

2. A relationship of commitment would mean *going beyond periodic acts of cooperation to sustained collaboration* based on a conviction that mission, if it is to be fully effective and faithful, requires the participation of the other. A quick word of background is needed to explain what I have in mind.

One of the most notable developments in ecumenical thought over the past half century is the shift, now widely embraced, to an understanding of mission as *missio Dei* — the mission of God. We used to talk about the churches' missions; now we speak of God's mission in which the church is privileged to participate. Under the old paradigm, *mission* was practically synonymous with evangelism, and even acts of service were stamped with the Christian label (usually the label of our particular branch of the Christian tree) in order to show that this was the work of the church. The concept of *missio Dei* focuses not on the actions of the church but on the One who sends us; and it widens the understanding of mission to include God's whole work of healing and liberation.

This approach to mission has obviously helped clear the way for cooperative activity, at least on occasion; but the question I am raising now is whether Christians can and should go further — to affirm that mission, which used to be aimed *at* Jews and other interfaith neighbors, should be done *with* them. Poverty or climate change or racism or war are not simply Christian problems! Indeed, it makes little sense to speak of the Christian response to such challenges, since they are too massive to be dealt with by any one faith community. If we believe that God's mission involves protecting the environment or acting on behalf of society's most vulnerable members, then our participation in that mission *demands* collaboration with Jewish and other interfaith partners. It is not just expedient but faithful to do so.

Of course, Jews (to focus again on that relationship) may see all of this differently. I believe that Christians, however, should welcome moving from cooperation to commitment, a level of relationship in which we would seek opportunities to do mission with Jewish organizations, nationally and locally. At the NCC, persons of other faiths have (at best) been "guests" at our assemblies. If we moved from cooperation to commitment, we would want them to be present as full partners in God's mission.

3. Perhaps most important, a relationship of commitment would mean *staying together even in the face of significant disagreement about matters of real importance.*[18] Over the past two decades, American Jews, with their obvious ties to the state of Israel, and mainline Christians, with their mission ties to Palestinian churches, have grown increasingly at odds over the Israeli-Palestinian conflict — to the point that some Jewish organizations have threatened to sever relations with churches that support certain Palestinian initiatives, no matter how nonviolent they may be. This has made it more difficult for those who care deeply about Jewish-Christian relations to talk frankly about the issues at stake.

But what if Christian and Jewish leaders were to declare, at the outset, their commitment to an enduring relationship, rooted in their recognition of a shared religious patrimony and fifty years of rapprochement? What if they were to acknowledge that, in some sense, a relationship to the other is part of their religious identity as children of one Creator who has made a lasting covenant with both? Far from sweeping disagreements under the rug, such a commitment would allow them to be addressed with complete honesty, but without the threat that one party or the other will leave the table.

Of course, security for Israelis, including Israeli Jews, and justice for Palestinians, including Palestinian Christians, are matters of great consequence. They touch on our identity as people of faith. But, speaking as a Christian, I am convinced that the church's relationship with Jews and Judaism is also crucial to Christian self-understanding. And I believe it is important and appropriate, therefore, to raise the possibility of thinking of this relationship in terms of commitment, not just cooperation.

18. See chapter 11.

CHAPTER 3

Is the Ecumenical Movement a Movement for Peace?

Forty years after its German publication, *And Yet It Moves* remains one of the most insightful books ever written about the ecumenical movement. Its author, German educator Ernst Lange, argues passionately in the book's closing chapter that "the ecumenical movement *is* a movement for peace."[1] Lange takes it as given that the church has a scriptural mandate to work for the peace of the human family — or, better, to participate in God's mission of peacemaking. And, like Martin Luther King Jr., he contends that the mind-boggling power of modern weaponry makes the division of humanity into warring groups, nations, and ideologies dangerously (disastrously!) obsolete.[2] The church, as an instrument of God's shalom, must proclaim *and demonstrate* the interdependence of the human family — and that is the very purpose of the church renewal movement we call "ecumenical." Ecumenism, Lange concludes, is "the way in which the Christian churches really serve the cause of peace."[3]

In this chapter I want to bolster both of Lange's claims: (1) that peacemaking is not simply one item on the ecumenical agenda (ecumenism *is* a movement for peace in human community), and (2) that the visible unity of the church, ecumenism's often-stated goal, is essential to the Christian witness for peace. Such claims must not be taken for granted. In the history

1. Ernst Lange, *And Yet It Moves*, trans. Edwin Robertson (Geneva: WCC, 1979), p. 147.

2. See Lange, *And Yet It Moves*, p. 160; Martin Luther King Jr., "A Christmas Sermon on Peace," in James M. Washington, ed., *A Testament of Hope: The Essential Writings and Speeches of Martin Luther King, Jr.* (New York: Harper Collins, 1986), p. 253.

3. Lange, *And Yet It Moves*, p. 147.

of the church, those who have emphasized peacemaking have often feared that unity would blunt the prophetic edge of their proclamation, while those who have emphasized unity have often feared that radical peacemaking would prove divisive. That's why the historic peace churches — Mennonites, Friends (Quakers), Brethren — have generally been sectarian, while churches inclined toward collaboration have generally left matters of war and peace to the individual conscience.

The ecumenical movement, at its best, has rejected that dichotomy. In the words of former World Council of Churches (WCC) General Secretary Konrad Raiser, the question of war and peace "is not an additional or an external concern that is thrust upon the churches seeking peacemaking and rebuilding communion among each other, but is integral to the emergence of the ecumenical impulse and the ecumenical movement."[4] And the realization of a common Christian position on war and peacemaking — or, at least, a convergence toward it — is one of the true, if underappreciated, triumphs of ecumenical dialogue.

Shaped by War

It is important to recall that the historical development of ecumenism has been decisively shaped by periods of intense international conflict. The Life and Work movement, one of the streams that formed the WCC, was born amid the debris of World War I. Those four years of carnage were, in effect, a Christian civil war — Protestant Britain, Roman Catholic France, and Orthodox Russia allied against Protestant Germany, Roman Catholic Austria, and Orthodox Bulgaria — with no mechanism or platform for bringing the churches together for dialogue and possible common witness. It was this lacuna that the Lutheran archbishop Nathan Söderblom and others sought to fill with their conferences on the life and work of Christian community. As the participants at the first conference (Stockholm, 1925) put it, "The world is too strong for a divided church."[5]

The World Council itself was formed during, and deeply influenced by, the German Church Struggle of the 1930s and, especially, by World War II.

4. Konrad Raiser, "Remarks to the Bienenberg Consultation," in Fernando Enns, Scott Holland, and Ann Riggs, eds., *Seeking Cultures of Peace* (Telford, Pa.: Cascadia Publishing, 2004), p. 20.

5. Quoted in Paul Abrecht, "Life and Work," in Nicholas Lossky et al., eds., *Dictionary of the Ecumenical Movement* (Geneva: WCC, 2002), p. 691.

The 1937 Oxford Conference on Church and Society, a conference that called for the establishment of the WCC, also made this seminal declaration: "If war breaks out, then pre-eminently the church must manifestly be the church, still united as the one Body of Christ, though the nations wherein it is planted fight each other. . . . The fellowship of prayer must at all costs remain unbroken."[6] Willem Visser 't Hooft, first general secretary of the WCC, called these sentences "the charter of the ecumenical movement"[7] and incorporated them into a letter sent to all members of the "World Council in process of formation" once war actually began. The letter also lamented how miserably the church had failed to be the church in the First World War, called on the churches not to present the war as a holy crusade, and urged Christian leaders to prepare for the future by "seeking to ascertain from fellow Christians in the opposing camp what terms of peace might create a lasting peace."[8]

The ecumenical movement was further defined by the Cold War, by the fact that, even at the height of nuclear tension, the Iron Curtain did not prevent regular contact between churches east and west. Ecumenical leaders repeatedly expressed a profound sense of relatedness in the face of political and military conflict. "I find," said the Norwegian bishop Eivind Berggrav to a meeting of the WCC Central Committee in the 1950s, "that the New Testament demands of me that I shall be willing to accept as a full brother in Christ a man who seems to me quite dangerous in his political or economic views."[9] A well-publicized demonstration of such relationship came when the Russian Orthodox Church joined the WCC at the council's assembly in 1961, the very eve of the Cuban missile crisis. This, said the assembly's delegates, is "a dramatic confirmation of our faith that God is holding his family together in spite of sin and complexity, and is a sign of hope for the world."[10]

A Growing Convergence

I want to approach this history from another direction. Over the centuries, Christians have not only found themselves on different sides of particular

6. J. H. Oldham, ed., *The Oxford Conference: Official Report* (Chicago: Willett and Clark, 1937), p. 47.

7. W. A. Visser 't Hooft, *Memoirs* (London: SCM Press, 1973), p. 73.

8. Visser 't Hooft, *Memoirs*, p. 110.

9. Quoted in Visser 't Hooft, *Memoirs*, p. 225.

10. W. A. Visser 't Hooft, ed., *The New Delhi Report: The Third Assembly of the World Council of Churches* (New York: Association Press, 1962), pp. 108-9.

conflicts, they have obviously disagreed on whether or not war is ever jus-
tifiable — to the point of clear division in the body of Christ. The Augsburg
Confession, to take only one example, states that "Christians may without
sin . . . punish evildoers with the sword, engage in just wars, and serve as
soldiers. We, therefore, condemn the Anabaptists who teach that these things
aren't Christian."[11]

These profound disagreements, even anathemas, were brought into the
modern ecumenical movement. The report from the Oxford conference of
1937 outlines "two widely divergent views regarding war, along with several
that are intermediate," but goes on to argue that the movement cannot rest
content with the cataloging of disputes.[12] The world situation demands the
articulation of common ground!

Somewhat astonishingly, common ground has, in fact, been discovered,
thanks to decades of ecumenical study, dialogue, and shared experience.
In what follows, I want to name five elements of this growing convergence.
It probably goes without saying that churches continue to disagree over
whether to support war or violent revolution as an option of last resort; but
these five "principles" still demonstrate the remarkable extent to which old
disputes have been overcome. Listing elements of convergence in this way
does not do justice to their historical context (which is always important);
but, in my judgment, these principles constitute a shared Christian position
that transcends their historical and political setting:

1. *"War is contrary to the will of God."*[13] Already at Oxford, the churches
had said together that war as a method of settling disputes is incompatible
with the teachings and example of our Lord, Jesus Christ. "No justification of
war must be allowed to conceal or minimize this fact."[14] But this eight-word
sentence from the report of the WCC's first assembly (Amsterdam, 1948),
repeated numerous times in subsequent statements, is even more pointed:
"War is contrary to the will of God." It may be that war is, at times, a necessary evil, but it is still "inherently evil"[15] — which means that Christians
should never identify warfare with the purposes of God. To put it another

11. Augsburg Confession, Article 16.
12. Oldham, ed., *The Oxford Conference*, pp. 162-67.
13. "The Church and the International Disorder," in W. A. Visser 't Hooft, ed., *Man's Disorder and God's Design: The Amsterdam Assembly Series* (New York: Harper and Brothers, 1949), p. 218.
14. Oldham, ed., *The Oxford Conference*, p. 162.
15. W. A. Visser 't Hooft, ed., *The Evanston Report: The Second Assembly of the World Council of Churches* (New York: Harper and Brothers, 1955), p. 132.

way, a "crusade" or "holy war" is not an acceptable Christian position. God's will is for shalom. No one should go to war in the name of God.

I need to reiterate that this is not a strictly pacifist position; and indeed, ecumenical conferences have not endorsed pacifism. For example, delegates to the WCC's ninth assembly in 2006 adopted a statement on the "Responsibility to Protect," affirming (through gritted teeth) that "the fellowship of churches is not prepared to say that it is never appropriate or never necessary to resort to the use of force for the protection of the vulnerable."[16] The focus of the statement, however, is on preventing such situations from arising (a point to which we will return), and the statement never suggests that God blesses such military intervention, no matter how well intentioned. Even Reinhold Niebuhr, an influential critic of pacifism, rebuked those who invoked divine guidance for the "ungodly" act of war. Presuming God's sanction for our violence, argued Niebuhr, is simply another form of sinful pride.[17] Because war is contrary to the will of God.

2. *"There are some forms of violence in which Christians may not participate and which the churches must condemn."*[18] This line comes from the report of a two-year study process — titled "Violence, Nonviolence, and the struggle for Social Justice" — that was commended to the churches by the WCC's Central Committee in 1973. The study was prompted, in large part, by efforts to oppose systemic racism in South Africa and the United States (King had been scheduled to preach at the council's fourth assembly in 1968) and remained the WCC's most substantial work on the subject until the Decade to Overcome Violence (DOV, 2000-10). Once again, the churches did not agree on whether violent resistance is ever appropriate or necessary in situations of oppression; but they did agree that some forms of violence must always be precluded, never to be endorsed by Christians. These include "the conquest of one people by another or the deliberate oppression of one class or race by another . . . torture in all forms, the holding of innocent hostages and the deliberate or indiscriminate killing of innocent non-combatants."[19]

This point undergirds the broad ecumenical denunciation of nuclear

16. Luis N. Rivera-Pagan, ed., *God, in Your Grace: Official Report of the Ninth Assembly of the World Council of Churches* (Geneva: WCC, 2007), p. 307.

17. See Reinhold Niebuhr, *The Nature and Destiny of Man*, vol. 1 (New York: Charles Scribner's Sons, 1941), pp. 283-84.

18. "Violence, Nonviolence and the Struggle for Social Justice," in Michael Kinnamon and Brian E. Cope, eds., *The Ecumenical Movement: An Anthology of Key Texts and Voices* (Grand Rapids: Eerdmans, 1977), p. 217.

19. Kinnamon and Cope, eds., *The Ecumenical Movement*, p. 217.

weapons. The strongest statement came from the WCC's assembly in 1983: "The production and deployment of nuclear weapons, as well as their use, constitute a crime against humanity."[20] Christians, said the assembly, should work for the elimination of these weapons and should refuse to participate in their manufacture. This concern receded as an ecumenical priority after 1989 (as if the threat posed by nuclear weapons had gone away!), but in recent years has again become a focus of attention.

3. *Nonviolent resistance is central to the way of peace.* This principle seems implicit in all of the others but is of such importance that it merits separate mention. The 1973 study acknowledged that, despite the example of the American civil rights movement, in which churches were highly involved, "far too little attention has been given by the church and by resistance movements to the methods and techniques of non-violence in the struggle for a just society."[21] Subsequent studies and assemblies, however, have commended the practice of nonviolent resistance, without overlooking the fact that it, too, is highly political and potentially co-opted. Such specific initiatives as the Ecumenical Accompaniment Program in Palestine and Israel reflect this growing, and shared, commitment. The formulation I have chosen — nonviolent resistance is central to the way of peace — is adapted from the final statement of the International Ecumenical Peace Convocation (IEPC), a conference culminating the Decade to Overcome Violence, in 2011.[22]

4. *Peace is inseparable from justice.* Ecumenical statements have approached this principle from different directions. For example, the WCC's Nairobi Assembly (1975) insisted that peace is foundational to justice, since militarization distorts social and economic priorities, taking the greatest toll on the poor;[23] while the following assembly in Vancouver (1983) stressed that "without justice for all everywhere, we shall never have peace anywhere"[24] — but the basic affirmation is that the two belong together. Thanks to the DOV, this affirmation has taken the form of a new paradigm beyond the old alternatives of just war and pacifism. The message from the IEPC puts

20. David Gill, ed., *Gathered for Life: The Official Report of the Sixth Assembly of the World Council of Churches* (Geneva: WCC, 1983), p. 137. Several U.S.-based denominations produced statements on nuclear weapons in the years following the WCC's assembly in 1983.

21. Kinnamon and Cope, eds., *The Ecumenical Movement*, p. 217.

22. "An Ecumenical Call to Just Peace," par. 9, at http://www.overcomingviolence.org/fileadmin/dov/files/iepc/resources/ECJustPeace_English.pdf.

23. See David M. Paton, ed., *Breaking Barriers: Nairobi 1975* (London: SPCK, 1976), pp. 124, 181.

24. Gill, ed., *Gathered for Life*, p. 132.

it directly: ". . . we are moving beyond the doctrine of just war towards a commitment to just peace."[25]

At the heart of the "just peace" paradigm is a simple but profound insight: It is not enough to react to the threat of war; the church, with the help of God, must be proactive in its efforts to change those conditions that set the stage for violence. The United Church of Christ theologian Susan Brooks Thistlethwaite, in an essay following 9-11, offers a concrete example of what this might mean for public policy. Afghanistan, as she puts it, needed a Marshall Plan after the period of Soviet occupation, but the U.S. and other wealthy countries did not act because Afghanistan didn't then seem vital to their national interests. "We let poverty and oppression rule," she writes, "and now we are reaping the results."[26] Similarly, working for peace in Iraq in 2003, while important, was too late. The church in 2003 needed to be working for peace in 2020 by addressing those issues — poverty, AIDS, illiteracy, international debt — that may well contribute to future conflict. Seen in this light, the decision to use armed force *always* represents a failure of governments — and churches — to work proactively for justice.

This concept of just peace, which is increasingly endorsed by the ecumenically-engaged churches, is a critique of both pacifism and just war. Violence, the churches now acknowledge, is not only a feature of war; it is embedded in the status quo, even when there is no apparent conflict. The Pax Romana, the "peace" maintained by the might of the Roman army, was hardly nonviolent for slaves or Jews or other persecuted people in the time of Jesus. Authentic peacemaking will seek to "unmask" such structural violence and to advocate vigorously on behalf of those victimized by it. A pacifism unattuned to this ongoing, often hidden warfare, a pacifism that is "an excuse to retreat from public responsibility into sectarian reservations of spiritual life,"[27] may actually be detrimental to the cause of peace.

On the other hand, an insistence that justice is a prerequisite for peace may simply be a new form of the just-war tradition. Justice and peace need to be held in dialectical tension if Christians are to avoid the divisive disputes of earlier generations.

25. "Glory to God and Peace on Earth: The Message of the International Ecumenical Peace Convocation," at http://www.overcomingviolence.org/en/resources-dov/wcc-resources/documents/presentations-speeches-messages/iepc-message.html.

26. Susan Brooks Thistlethwaite, "New Wars, Old Wineskins," in Jon L. Berquist, ed., *Strike Terror No More* (St. Louis: Chalice Press, 2002), p. 265.

27. This comes from a study paper prepared for the NCC's Centennial Assembly in 2010. It can be found at http://www.ncccusa.org/witnesses2010/christian-understanding-of-war.pdf.

5. *"Reconciliation stands at the heart of the gospel message."*[28] This may sound obvious to anyone who has pondered such biblical texts as 2 Corinthians 5:16-20; but the emphasis on reconciliation at recent ecumenical conferences has been touted as nothing less than "a new paradigm for mission."[29] It implies the church's involvement with perpetrators as well as victims, and its responsibility to participate in the reconstruction of societies (e.g., Rwanda or Liberia) on the other side of war or the revolutionary struggle against oppression.

The idea that peacemaking should "aim at the conversion and not the destruction of the opponent," looking toward the possibility of restored relationship, was already present in the 1973 report on violence and nonviolence.[30] Over the following three decades, however, ecumenical discussion focused more on liberation than reconciliation. Current proponents of the new paradigm stress that reconciliation, if it is authentic, must include a concern for justice; but, seen in historical context, there is a different tone — symbolized by the move from the WCC's Program to *Combat* Racism to its Decade to *Overcome* Violence (subtitled "Churches Seeking Reconciliation and Peace").

Reconciliation truly emerged as a dominant theme at the 2005 Conference on World Mission and Evangelism, in Athens, from which my formulation of this principle — "reconciliation stands at the heart of the gospel message" — is taken. The message of that meeting is unmistakable: The church is called beyond political action to participation in the healing mission of God — creating safe, hospitable spaces where truth can be spoken and heard, helping to rebuild relationships, and fostering the sort of tough-minded forgiveness (not forgetfulness) that makes a different kind of future possible for both victim and offender. We hear in this the clear influence of the "truth and reconciliation" processes that have had such impact, with church leadership, in South Africa, Central America, and other parts of the world.

Embodying Shalom

I hope that the above five principles, now widely endorsed by churches involved in the ecumenical movement, demonstrate both how central

28. "A Letter from Athens," in Jacques Matthey, ed., *Come Holy Spirit, Heal and Reconcile! Report of the WCC Conference on World Mission and Evangelism* (Geneva: WCC, 2008), p. 325.

29. Robert Schreiter, "Reconciliation as a New Paradigm for Mission," in *Come Holy Spirit*, pp. 213-19.

30. Kinnamon and Cope, eds., *The Ecumenical Movement*, p. 217.

peace is to the movement's agenda and how extensive the convergence is toward a common Christian position — a convergence every bit as significant, in my judgment, as the widely celebrated agreement on justification by faith. There is, however, a sixth principle running throughout modern ecumenism that must be highlighted because it seems so often overlooked: *The unity of the church is itself crucial to the Christian witness for peace.*

Part of the point is sociological: Divisions in the body of Christ frequently exacerbate political conflicts and hinder effective peacemaking, which must be undertaken ecumenically. The Methodist or Greek Orthodox response to war makes as little sense as the Presbyterian or Roman Catholic response to climate change! Such issues are simply too large to be tackled in denominational isolation.

The real point, however, is more theological: God's gift of reconciliation is for the world; but the church, in the words of the apostle Paul, is entrusted with this message of reconciliation (2 Cor. 5:18-20). And, as Paul's letters make clear, the church is to deliver the message not just by what it *says* or even by what it *does,* but by what it *is* — by the way its members live with one another. Ecumenical conferences have repeatedly affirmed that the church is to be a sign, a demonstration project, of God's intent for all creation, which we often sum up with the Hebrew word *shalom.* The church isn't just the bearer of the message of reconciliation; it is, or is to be, the message embodied.

To put it negatively, the message of peace is constantly undercut by the sorry state of the messengers — still divided by race, neglecting the needs of sisters and brothers who worship God incarnate under different labels, acting more like competing corporations than members of a single body. We're unable to break bread together at the table of reconciliation, failing to recognize our connection to followers of Christ who live in nations that our nation calls "enemy." That is why a National Council of Churches consultation in 1995 declared that "the divisions in the Body of Christ in the world are a counter-witness to the peace sought and proclaimed by the church as the follower of the Prince of Peace who prayed that his disciples might be one."[31] The churches, said participants in the consultation, must repent of past antagonism toward one another, seek common ground through hearing one another's histories, and recognize that "the

31. Jeffrey Gros and John D. Rempel, eds., *The Fragmentation of the Church and Its Unity in Peacemaking* (Grand Rapids: Eerdmans, 2001), p. 221.

movement toward unity . . . is itself a sign and model of their peacemaking vocation."[32]

I certainly don't mean to suggest that holding unity and peace together is easy! There are times when, in the course of working for peace with justice, Christians must take sides against sisters and brothers in the church. To take an extreme example, the ecumenical movement's outspoken struggle against the violence of the apartheid system caused some Reformed churches in South Africa to withdraw from the WCC, and it became the focus of criticism for many others.[33] But even when taking sides, our understanding of church must be shaped more by theology than politics. Even in such moments, we must recognize that the "they" we oppose are, in some fundamental sense, "we" — because the story by which we live tells us that we have been linked in communion beyond human agreement. This, itself, is a profound testimony to God's shalom.[34]

Practicing Peace

It is now time to acknowledge the obvious: Despite the fact that ecumenically engaged churches are forging a once-unthinkable consensus regarding war and peace, the churches' witness in times of conflict remains ineffective. Dr. King, though phrasing it as a question, was far more blunt: "What more pathetically reveals the irrelevance of the church in present-day world affairs than its witness against war?"[35]

One reason is that numerous churches (generally speaking, conservative evangelical and Pentecostal) have not participated in — or, consequently, embraced — the convergence noted above. As a result, it is not un-

32. Gros and Rempel, eds., *The Fragmentation of the Church*, pp. 221-22.

33. Another example is the German Church Struggle of the 1930s and participation in World War II. Ecumenical leaders generally called on the WCC, then in process of formation, to stand firmly against Nazism and to call the churches to support the struggle against it, while still working together for eventual reconciliation. One of these leaders was Dietrich Bonhoeffer. The ecumenical church, he wrote, "cannot just say, 'There should really be no war, but there are necessary wars' and leave the application of this principle to each individual. It should be able to say quite definitely: 'Engage in this war' or 'Do not engage in this war.' " Dietrich Bonhoeffer, *No Rusty Swords*, ed. Edwin H. Robertson (New York: Harper and Row, 1965), pp. 162-63.

34. See chapter 6.

35. From "A Knock at Midnight" at http://mlk-kpp01.stanford.edu/index.php/kingpapers/article/a_knock_at_midnight/.

usual to see the spectacle of some church leaders opposing, while others are supporting, impending combat on the part of their nation. Another reason, however, is that the official teachings of the churches, certainly including their ecumenical commitments, are too lacking in authority to shape the opinions and behavior of people in the pews. And without congregational investment, church statements "from the top" have little influence on public policy.

In such a situation, the churches may need to focus less on top-down pronouncements and more on programs of congregational formation.[36] More specifically, I recommend promotion of the following corporate "disciplines," which, if practiced, may help form a peacemaking sensibility in local communities.

1. *Pray on a regular basis for those regarded as enemies by our nation or group.* Scripture is clear about the importance of this for individual Christians; but the injunction in Matthew 5 to pray for our enemies surely applies to communities as well. "The churches," said the delegates at the WCC's first assembly (Amsterdam, 1948), "must teach the duty of love and prayer for the enemy in time of war and of reconciliation between victim and vanquished after the war."[37] One reason, of course, is that many of our nation's enemies will likely be Christians to whom we are related in the one body of Christ. In the words of the Oxford conference (1937), "if Christians in warring nations prayed according to the pattern of prayer given by their Lord, they will never be 'praying against' one another."[38] Beyond this, *every* neighbor, seen in scriptural perspective, is an infinitely valued child of God. Prayer for enemies is a powerful sign and instrument of this human unity that is at the heart of the gospel — and it is central to the vision of the ecumenical movement.

2. *Practice peace in our own congregations, especially by committing ourselves to seek relationship with people we prefer to avoid.* It is important to pray for enemies in distant places; but, to paraphrase 1 John 4, how can we speak of relationship with people we can't see if we can't demonstrate relationship with people we see every week? The two groups in the church that are most important for me to engage, writes Barbara Wheeler, are those I have injured

36. Ans van der Bent reaches a similar conclusion in his chapter on "Peace and Disarmament" in *Commitment to God's Word: A Concise Critical Survey of Ecumenical Social Thought* (Geneva: WCC, 1995), pp. 107-19.

37. Visser 't Hooft, ed., *Man's Disorder*, p. 219.

38. Oldham, ed., *The Oxford Conference*, p. 167. A good tool for this practice is the ecumenical prayer cycle *In God's Hands* (Geneva: WCC, 2006).

and those who most oppose my views.[39] Many of us spend most of our time in church with like-minded friends, people we would hang out with in other settings. This, however, obscures the church's potential as a community of reconciliation and sign of God's will for peace.

3. *Seek partnership with a nearby congregation that historically has taken a different approach to matters of war and peace.* Learn more about that history, including past persecution. Find out what drives that church's convictions about peace. And then study together some of the ecumenical statements referred to in this chapter.

4. *Join with other congregations in a local activity that counters violence.* One example is the ecumenical effort to reduce gun violence through participation in such organizations as Heeding God's Call. U.S. Christians can defend the Second Amendment right to bear arms and still be appalled (outraged!) by the senseless status quo in which an American child is twelve times more likely to be killed by gunfire than a child in the next twenty-five largest industrialized countries combined! This, however, is only one possible issue related to peace. A congregation should decide on the one that is most appropriate, most needed, in its setting and get involved.

A passionate, sustained commitment to peacemaking is often associated with only one segment of Christian community, namely the historic peace churches. "Another peace protest? It must be those Quakers or Mennonites or Brethren!"

What I have tried to show, however, is that costly, insistent peacemaking is *not* limited to these few. It is the mission of the ecumenical church. *All* churches should see themselves as peace churches. And all churches should recognize that participation in the ecumenical movement is an essential way for them to live out this calling. Commitment to peace is common ground on which the churches can unite. And this unity is, in turn, a sign of the peace that God gives and promises.

---

39. Barbara G. Wheeler, "True Confession: A Presbyterian Dissenter Thinks About the Church," in *The Church and Its Unity,* Church Issues Series, No. 1 (Presbyterian Church [USA] Office of Theology and Worship, 1999), pp. 15-16.

CHAPTER 4

What Can the Churches Say Together About the Church?

The central issue for the ecumenical movement is the nature and purpose of the church. Discussions of what is required for Christian unity, and what unity might look like, are discussions about the essence of the church. Dialogues focused on sacraments or ministry or ways of making decisions deal with practices and structures that help define the church. Acts of shared witness and service undertaken through councils of churches reflect implicit convictions about how the church relates to the world. A roll call of ecumenical participants — Orthodox, Roman Catholic, Anglican, historic Protestant, Anabaptist, Pentecostal — is shorthand for divergent conceptions of what the church is and what it is for.

Thus, it is a source of real joy — and, I think, encouragement — to note just how much the churches have said together, as a result of ecumenical dialogue, about the church's essential nature and its participation in the mission of God. In this chapter, I want to share this encouragement by identifying twelve areas of ecclesiological convergence (i.e., twelve points of growing agreement about the nature and purpose of the church).

It is possible, of course, to claim too much. Churches may affirm the points that follow but mean quite different things by their affirmations, since they are still operating out of divergent ecclesial paradigms. I am convinced, however, that it is also possible to claim too little. These areas of convergence show that churches are now thinking *together* about what the church is and does. This is — at least, potentially — a real breakthrough for the ecumenical movement, a significant contribution not only to the search for Christian unity, but also to the renewal of existing churches here and now.

For those interested in more extensive study of this emerging "ecumen- ical ecclesiology," several fine resources are available.[1] My intent here is sim- ply to name, as clearly as I can, various areas of convergence, and to suggest, as briefly as I can, why they are important. Any such listing is bound to be somewhat arbitrary; since the points intersect and can be subdivided, I could easily have had six or sixteen. My hope, however, is that this list of twelve is both memorable and clarifying.

In putting this together, I have drawn primarily on five texts developed over the past thirty years by the World Council of Churches (WCC), espe- cially its Commission on Faith and Order:

- *Baptism, Eucharist and Ministry* (BEM, 1982);
- "The Unity of the Church as Koinonia: Gift and Calling" (Canberra Statement), a statement adopted by the WCC's Canberra Assembly (1991);
- "The Nature and Mission of the Church" (NMC), a study document pro- duced by Faith and Order and sent to the churches for response (2005);
- "Called to Be the One Church" (Porto Alegre), an "invitation" to ec- clesiological dialogue, sent to the churches by the WCC's Porto Alegre Assembly (Brazil, 2006); and
- "The Church," a substantial rewriting of NMC, taking account of re- sponses to the earlier text, intended for consideration at the Council's 2013 assembly in Busan, South Korea.[2]

Excellent work has been done on this topic by various bilateral dialogues (i.e., dialogues between two churches or church traditions), and I will make occasional reference to these theological conversations. Such work, however, is necessarily particular to the churches involved, while Faith and Order includes theologians from a wide range of churches on six continents. I will

1. See, e.g., the essays in Gesa Thiessen, ed., *Ecumenical Ecclesiology: Unity, Diversity and Otherness in a Fragmented World* (London: T. and T. Clark, 2009); and G. R. Evans, *The Church and the Churches: Toward an Ecumenical Ecclesiology* (Cambridge: Cambridge Uni- versity Press, 2002).

2. The first four of these texts are easily accessible online. BEM and the Canberra State- ment are also in Michael Kinnamon and Brian E. Cope, eds., *The Ecumenical Movement: An Anthology of Key Texts and Voices* (Geneva: WCC, 1997), pp. 176-200 and 124-25. The fifth text, at the time of this writing (March 2012), is only in draft form. References to these five documents are included in the body of this essay. Numbers in the citations refer to numbered paragraphs in the texts.

also make reference to two other WCC studies: "The Community of Women and Men in the Church" and "Ecclesiology and Ethics." Some themes from these studies have found their way into the assembly and commission documents; but, in my judgment, their influence should be felt more widely and deeply.

Points of Agreement

Even as I write the preceding paragraphs, I can sense an elephant in the room. In these early years of the twenty-first century, certainly in the United States, "church" has become for many people either negative or irrelevant. For one thing, the individualism of North American culture means that religion has become, even for many who identify themselves as Christian, a private quest for meaning, largely divorced from community worship, formation, and mission. I recently heard singer Rosanne Cash, interviewed on National Public Radio, boil her religious commitment down to key personal values — compassion, non-violence — adding, "I don't need to play team sports in religion." It is a statement shared, I am sure, by lots of people in this country who believe in God and think of themselves as "spiritual."

Beyond that, church is now associated, for many persons, with exclusion, not gracious welcome; with an inward focus, not expansive care for the poor or for creation; with corporate-like structures and staid rituals, not passionate worship and difference-making mission; with cover-up of abusive behavior, not concern for those who are abused. In the words of theologian Daniel Migliore, "'Jesus yes, church no' nicely summarizes the anger and frustration that discussion of the church frequently arouses." And ecclesiology, the church's efforts at theological self-definition, is also not much in favor. The famous motto of early ecumenical leaders — "Let the church be the church!" — writes Migliore, is actually "a summons to the church to stop preening itself with all sorts of metaphysical compliments without any corresponding social reality and praxis."[3]

I acknowledge (who doesn't?) that there is truth in these critiques. Still, it is also true that the church — presented with such images as the People of God, the Body of Christ, and the Community of the Holy Spirit — is a central theme of the New Testament, a crucial dimension of the Good

3. Daniel L. Migliore, *Faith Seeking Understanding* (Grand Rapids: Eerdmans, 1991), pp. 185, 188.

News itself. Can the ecumenical movement help Christians recover the importance of the church? Can this emerging ecumenical ecclesiology be an instrument for renewing the churches' life and witness? I urge readers to keep these questions in mind when considering the following common affirmations:

1. *The church is, most fundamentally, a gift of God, a creation of the Word of God and of the Holy Spirit.* This theological affirmation counters the implicit ecclesiology of some churches, and promoted by the entire culture, that the church is a purely human organization, a voluntary association of like-minded believers. The point is spelled out clearly in NMC: "The Church is not merely the sum of individual believers in communion with God, nor primarily the mutual communion of individual believers among themselves. It is their common partaking in the life of God, who as Trinity is the source and focus of communion" (NMC, 13).

This is not to deny that the church *is* a human community, but to acknowledge that it is much, much more — and this acknowledgement has enormous implications. If the church is God's, then *we* don't set its boundaries or determine its entrance requirements. If the church is God's, then its purpose is not simply to meet our spiritual needs but to gather us for costly discipleship on behalf of God's agenda. "As a divinely established communion, the church belongs to God and does not exist for itself . . ." ("The Church," 12).

This also means that the essential attributes of the church, discussed below, flow from God and are not simply the product of human industry, let alone human merit. The church is holy because God, its source of life, is the Holy One whose ever-new offer of forgiveness enables the repentance and reform of its members. The church is catholic because of the abundant goodness of God that empowers it to transcend worldly barriers. The church is apostolic because it is created and sustained by the Word of God, to which the apostles bore definitive witness, and because, like the apostles, it participates in the divine mission of proclamation and service. The church is one-in-diversity because that is God's essential nature ("The Church," 25). Wherever and whenever we see these attributes — oneness, holiness, catholicity, and apostolicity — in the actual life of Christian community, it is not human achievement we celebrate, but God's gift for which we give thanks.

2. *The nature of the church is best expressed as "koinonia,"* which is why, in the words of NMC, this biblical concept "has become central in the quest for a common understanding of the church and its visible unity" (NMC, 24). *Koinonia* is usually translated as "communion," "fellowship," "sharing," or "participation," but the Greek word has resonance beyond its English equiv-

alents. It derives not from sociological experience (e.g., that communion is "good for us"), but from faith in God whose very being, Christians confess, is *koinonia*. God, in Christian teaching, is not One who relates, but One — Father, Son, and Holy Spirit — who *is* relationship. And this leads to an understanding of church that, once again, counters the individualization of our culture and era by insisting that the very fabric of the church is relatedness.

It is not coincidental, I think, that *koinonia* began to appear in the ecumenical vocabulary in 1961, when, at its New Delhi Assembly, the WCC adopted a trinitarian affirmation as its basis for membership.[4] The report from that assembly includes a famous description of Christian unity as "a fully committed fellowship." "The word 'fellowship' (koinonia) has been chosen," according to the report, "because it describes what the church truly is. 'Fellowship' clearly implies that the church is not merely an institution or organization. It is a fellowship of those who are called together by the Holy Spirit and in baptism confess Christ as Lord and Savior. They are thus 'fully committed' to him and to one another."[5] This is a vital corrective to overly static or institutionalized conceptions of the church, a way of saying that the unity we seek is not organizational merger but a deepening and expanding quality of life together.

Koinonia will figure in much of what follows, so here I will add only one other point. The apostle Paul uses the same word, *koinonia,* when he speaks of participation in the Lord's Supper (1 Cor. 10:16-17) and when he urges sharing on behalf of the poor in Jerusalem (Rom. 15:26-27). As a result, the idea of *koinonia* contributes to a more integrated ecclesiology. Worship and mission, to take that example, are intimately related in any proper understanding of the church.

3. *Koinonia is expressed in the relationship of the local and universal church;* or, to say it more directly, the universal church is a communion of local churches, in each of which the fullness of the church resides. Each gathered community of believers, in which the gospel is preached and the sacraments celebrated, in which Christ dwells by faith, is truly church — but not the whole of it. In the words from Porto Alegre, "Each church fulfills its catholicity when it is in communion with other churches," a communion marked by mutual accountability (Porto Alegre, 6).

4. This point, part of a fine discussion of *koinoina,* was made by John Zizioulas (Metropolitan John of Pergamon) at the Fifth World Conference on Faith and Order. See "The Church as Communion," in Thomas F. Best and Günther Gassmann, eds., *On the Way to Fuller Koinonia* (Geneva: WCC, 1994), pp. 103-4.

5. In Kinnamon and Cope, eds., *The Ecumenical Movement,* p. 89.

This may seem, at first glance, a rather esoteric discussion. However, given the tendency of some Christians to act as if the church were only their congregation, with little concern for other Christian communities, and the tendency of some church leaders down through the centuries to sound as if the universal church dominates the local, with little respect for local differences, this point of agreement is of real significance. One of the bilateral dialogues, the Anglican-Roman Catholic Consultation in the U.S., names what is at stake with particular clarity:

> The church is . . . *both* local and universal. The church local is not merely a subdivision of the church universal, nor is the church universal merely an aggregate of the local churches. Each is fully interdependent with the other. When the balance between local and universal is upset, there is danger for the church's institutional embodiment. . . . When, however, the proper balance is kept, the church's real catholicity is more easily seen, because the church appears as a communion of communities whose very diversity manifests the riches of the one faith in the one God through the one Christ.[6]

4. This leads directly to the fourth point: *The church is inherently one. Division not only contradicts the church's witness to the reconciling love of Christ, it is a denial of the church's very nature.* The "Message" from the WCC's first assembly (Amsterdam, 1948) says it succinctly: "Christ has made us His own and He is not divided."

Of course, bodies that lay claim to the name Christian *are*, empirically, divided — thereby giving rise to the irony that drives the ecumenical movement. Unity, as the Canberra Statement puts it, is both a gift and a calling as those who confess a common Lord seek to become what they are: the one body of Christ.

This point has been made so often in ecumenical settings — and its implications for the church's presence in a fragmented world are so obvious — that I will add only one observation from Porto Alegre: Given the church's inherent oneness, even denominations that are not yet able to share the eucharist can and should express their relatedness by praying for one another, sharing resources, assisting one another in times of need, making decisions

---

6. "Agreed Report on the Local/Universal Church" (November 15, 1999), at sccb.org/beliefs-and-teachings/ecumenical-and-interreligious/ecumenical/anglican/local-universal-church.cfm.

together whenever possible, working together for a more just and peaceful society, and generally refusing to say, "I have no need of you" (Porto Alegre, 7). Such actions are a sign that unity is the church's essential condition, division the aberration.

5. To make explicit what has been implied, *the inherent unity of the church is, itself, inherently diverse.* Indeed, the church's interrelated diversity is essential to its wholeness. Scriptural images such as the "body of Christ" show that difference, far from being a threat to oneness, is a condition of it. While all of the conciliar texts make this point, I will turn again to a bilateral dialogue for a helpful summary:

> Unity in Christ does not exist despite and in opposition to diversity, but is given with and in diversity. Because this diversity corresponds with the many gifts of the Holy Spirit to the church, it is a concept of fundamental ecclesial importance, with relevance to all aspects of the life of the church, and is not a mere concession to theological pluralism. Both the unity and diversity of the church are ultimately grounded in the communion of God the Holy Trinity.[7]

It should go without saying (although Christians have often denied it!) that the church encompasses the rich human variety of race, ethnicity, and culture. Our texts, however, go beyond that. To paraphrase the statement from Porto Alegre, there is one apostolic faith, which is expressed through legitimately different formulations; one life in Christ, which is built up through different ministries and gifts of the Spirit; one hope, which finds expression in different human expectations (Porto Alegre, 5). No one envisions a uniform church! But how we determine the limits of such diversity is clearly a question at the heart of the ongoing ecumenical conversation. What our texts suggest is that diversity is illegitimate when, and only when, it disrupts our communion and makes impossible the common confession of Jesus Christ as Lord and Savior (Canberra, 2.2).

6. *The church's unity is not simply a matter of invisible, spiritual relationship, as evangelical Christians sometimes claim, but must find visible expression in order "that the world may believe"* (John 17:21). According to its constitution, the first purpose of the WCC is "to call the churches to the goal

---

7. The *Porvoo Common Statement,* conversations between the British and Irish Anglican churches and the Nordic and Baltic Lutheran churches, quoted in Veli Matti Kärkkäinen, *An Introduction to Ecclesiology* (Downers Grove, Ill.: InterVarsity Press, 2002), p. 85.

of *visible* unity in one faith and in one eucharistic fellowship." The opposite of visible unity is visible disunity, and this obviously does not bear witness to God's power to reconcile those who are estranged from God and one another.

Actually, a better way to make this point, consistent with Augustine and the Protestant Reformers, would be to say that there is only one church, which is, at the same time, both visible and invisible. When Christians forget that there is an invisible fellowship known only to God, they are tempted to claim that their community is *the* church or that they know the church's true boundaries. An overemphasis on the invisible church, however, has also contributed to ecclesial divisions, with groups splitting from other parts of the visible body in the name of a true, if unseen, fellowship. The visible church, containing the faithful and the lukewarm, is not a perfect embodiment of the invisible church, but neither are the two separable.

7. There is now broad agreement, certainly in the documents we are examining, on *a short list of "tangible signs of the new life of communion"* (NMC, 32):

- shared confession of the apostolic faith (a mutual recognition that previously divided churches are confessing the same triune God, even when using different formulations);
- mutual recognition that, through baptism, Christians in the various churches are members together in the one body of Christ;
- shared celebration of the eucharist;
- mutual recognition of the validity of the ministries authorized by the previously divided churches;
- ability to meet, when needed, in order to make decisions together; and
- common mission, witnessing to the gospel of God's grace and serving all in need.

This list is of great importance because it constitutes a shared vision of what unity would look like and, thus, gives shape to the ecumenical agenda. There are many other areas of ecumenical dialogue, including such things as the relationship of Christians to interfaith neighbors, the elements of vital Christian worship, education in the life of the church, the tension between evangelism and advocacy for peace and justice, and the theological understanding of hope. No one, I trust, denies that such matters, and many others, are of real significance; but faithful Christians can disagree about them and still experience the *koinonia* that is our gift and calling. By contrast, the inability to break bread together or the failure to recognize one another's ministries as true ministries of Word and sacrament are not just examples of diversity; they are signs of division. The items on this list are fundamental bonds of communion. For unity to be substantive, we dare require no less — but we also need require no more.

8. *The discussion of "koinonia" points toward a ministry that serves the unity of the community while also being part of it.* Through their participation in Christ, all Christians are part of a royal priesthood; but that by no means negates the need for a representative ministry that builds up the body by preaching the Word, celebrating the sacraments, and providing guidance in mission. The most recent of our conciliar documents, "The Church," offers a clear summary of this convergence:

> All members of the body, ordained and lay, are interrelated. Ordained ministers remind the community of its dependence on Jesus Christ, who is the source of its unity and mission, even as they understand their own ministry as dependent on Him. At the same time, they can fulfill their calling only in and for the Church; they need its recognition, support, and encouragement ("The Church," 18).

It is no secret that "episcopal ministry" and "apostolic succession" have been major sticking points in ecumenical dialogue. I will certainly not suggest that all disputes over these matters have been resolved. I do want to note, however, the growing acknowledgement that the church needs a ministry of "oversight" (Greek, *episkopé*) in order to help preserve its unity and its fidelity to the faith Christians receive from the apostles. *Koinonia* means relationship with the disciples who have gone before and those who are yet to come, as well as with our contemporaries. Thus, a ministry of oversight (usually associated with the office of bishop) that stands in a line of succession from the apostles is now widely recognized as a valued sign, though not a guarantee, of continuity in the church's faith, worship, and mission — as a vital means for transmitting the church's apostolic tradition (BEM, M34, 37-38).

I am glad for these affirmations; but, in my judgment, much more is at stake in the ecumenical conversation about ministry. For those churches tempted to make the clergy an exalted caste, the ecumenical convergence is a reminder that ordained ministry can fulfill its calling "only in and for the church." For those churches tempted to regard ministry as something done by "experts" specially trained to accomplish it, the ecumenical convergence is a reminder that all are marked for ministry through baptism. For those churches tempted to think about ministry in secular terms, as a matter of organizational problem solving and institutional maintenance, the ecumenical convergence is a reminder that the church needs spiritual leaders and is not a business run by CEOs.

9. Authority is one of the toughest issues in ecumenical discussion, but there *is* biblically grounded agreement that *"the authority of the church comes from her Lord and Head, Jesus Christ"* ("The Church," 50), the one who "came not to be served but to serve, and to offer his life" for others (Mark 10:45). This means that authority, in gospel perspective, must be distinguished from mere power. The exercise of authority in the church may well call for obedience, "but such a call is meant to be welcomed with voluntary cooperation and consent, since its aim is to assist believers in growing to full maturity in Christ" ("The Church," 53).

There are twin dangers, clearly named in BEM, that need to be avoided. On the one hand, "authority cannot be exercised without regard for the community" (BEM, M16 [commentary]). The character of the church as *koinonia* means that authority, in the words of NMC, is "relational and interdependent" (NMC, 106). Decisions made by church leaders, if they are to have authority, must be "received," affirmed, and enacted by the faithful. On the other hand, authority exercised in the church cannot be "dependent on the common opinion of the community" (BEM, M16 [commentary]). Leaders are called to proclaim the Word of God, to determine and declare what the community needs, not just what it wants.

Getting this balance right is enormously important — and very difficult! There is certainly no shortage of examples in which church leaders wield power in ways that harm the community rather than build it up in love. Such studies as "The Community of Women and Men in the Church" challenge what many identify as male models of power, calling for a "church in the round," in which leadership is more collaborative than has often been true in the past.[8] At the same time, Christians are aware that fidelity to God's will requires discernment rooted in prayer, knowledge of Scripture, and understanding of tradition, not just a democratic process. This seems especially pertinent in a culture in which authority is located in the self and the very ideas of obedience and accountability are suspect.

---

8. See Constance F. Parvey, ed., *The Community of Women and Men in the Church* (Geneva: WCC, 1983). A good summary of the issues is found in Mary Tanner, "The Decade of Churches in Solidarity with Women: The Ecclesiological Challenges," in *One in Christ*, 35 (1999): 101-8.

I must admit that authority is a topic that has received far more extensive treatment in bilateral dialogues than in conciliar texts. After all, when council membership ranges from Orthodox to Baptist, authority is bound to be a neuralgic subject. Still, I believe that the convergence sketched in above is substantial enough to deserve serious consideration.

10. *The church is, by its very nature, "missionary" — called and sent by God to serve the world God so loves and to be a witness to God's coming reign* (NMC, 9). Mission is not simply something the church *does* (as if the church got to set its own agenda!); it is *part of God's very being* in which the church, as a divinely established communion, is privileged to participate. A church that does not regard mission as integral to its life is not the church of God who is in Jesus Christ.

One of the biggest divisions in the contemporary church — a division that runs within as well as between communions — is between those who emphasize evangelism when speaking of mission and those who emphasize work for justice and peace. Our conciliar texts, "The Church" being a good example, resist such bifurcation:

> The Church's mission in the world is to proclaim to all people, in word and deed, the Good News of salvation in Jesus Christ. Evangelization is thus the foremost task of the Church in obedience to the command of Jesus. The Church is called by Christ in the Holy Spirit to bear witness to the Father's reconciliation, healing, and transformation of creation. Thus, a constitutive aspect of evangelization is the promotion of justice and peace ("The Church," 62).

NMC certainly reflects the thrust of conciliar ecumenism over the past half century in its claim that "faith impels [Christian communities] to work for a more just social order, in which the goods of this earth, destined for the use of all, may be more justly shared . . . [and to] advocate peace, especially by seeking to overcome the causes of war" (NMC, 112). *Koinonia* is not only a matter of shared confession and common worship, but also of shared moral values derived from the gospel. As the WCC's "Ecclesiology and Ethics" study points out, the church is not constituted by the moral activities of its members (we are justified by grace through faith); but Christian faith should nonetheless be embodied in a corporate discipleship that resists threats to human life and all creation.[9]

9. See the report "Costly Unity," par. 7.2, at http://www.oikoumene.org/en/resources/

11. All of our texts insist that *the church, as God's creation, is a sign, a demonstration project, of what God intends for the salvation of the world* (Porto Alegre, 10; Canberra, 1.1). It is — is called to be — a "foretaste" of the day, promised in Scripture, when all creation will be brought into the fullness of communion with its Creator.

In this sense, the church is an eschatological reality, already anticipating the reign of God. At the same time, the church is clearly an historical reality, "exposed to the ambiguities of all human history and therefore [in need of] constant repentance and renewal in order to respond fully to its vocation" (NMC, 48). This paradoxical situation must be stated carefully: The church is, by its very nature, one; and yet it is marked by real divisions. The church is holy; and yet there is sin, individual and corporate, in its history. The church is catholic; and yet the wholeness of the gospel is frequently not preached or embodied by its members. The church is apostolic; and yet the church is not always faithful to the testimony of the apostles. Thus, it lives, only and always, by God's gracious forgiveness (NMC, 53-56).

12. The church exists "to serve in God's work of reconciliation and for the praise and glory of God" (NMC, 8). This is the first word and the last.

I hope this all-too-brief summary of what the churches have said together about the church has been useful and encouraging. There are, of course, numerous issues that require further study and dialogue, including the relationship between the institutional dimension of the church and the work of the Holy Spirit, the limits of legitimate diversity in regard to cultural expression, and the role of primacy in the church's conciliar decision making (often associated with the ministry of the Pope, the Bishop of Rome).[10]

In my judgment, however, what is most needed now is for the results of the growing convergence set forth in this chapter to make a substantive, tangible difference in the way Christians actually live as church. The Canberra Statement is more direct: "Churches have failed to draw the consequences for their life from the degree of communion they have already experienced and the agreements already achieved. They have remained satisfied to co-exist in division" (Canberra, 1.3).

Taking these twelve points seriously could help us, first, to recognize the

documents/wcc-commissions/faith-and-order-commission/vi-church-and-world-unity-and-the-life-of-the-church-in-the-world/ecclesiology-and-ethics/costly-unity.html. See also NMC, 113.

10. A more extensive list of such issues is found in Geoffrey Wainwright, "Church," in Nicholas Lossky et al., eds., *Dictionary of the Ecumenical Movement* (Geneva: WCC, 2002), p. 185.

presence of the one church of Jesus Christ in each other's particular churches, and thus advance the cause of unity. And it could help us, second, promote the renewal of our own church's structures, practices, and understandings. I strongly urge churches to make study of this convergence a part of their educational programs, and councils of churches to make study of it a major part of their agendas.

CHAPTER 5

What Can the Churches Say Together About the Environment?

It is not the purpose of this chapter to sound the alarm on climate change or other examples of threat to the natural environment. That has already been done many times. For example, regular reports from the United Nations Environment Programme carefully document such things as the substantial loss of biodiversity, the extensive degradation of useable land, the decline in available fresh water, and the increase in the earth's surface temperature (which impacts all of the other challenges). Unless one is ideologically resistant to the results of scientific study, it is hard to deny that we are in the midst of an environmental crisis "due to human activities in an increasingly globalized, industrialized, and interconnected world."[1]

The purpose of this chapter, rather, is to take note of the ecumenical convergence on this subject in order to encourage even greater church commitment to protection of the natural environment, both locally and globally. The ecological crisis is certainly not good news; but it *is* good news that Orthodox, Roman Catholic, and Protestant churches, including some who identify themselves as evangelical, now affirm a set of common principles that can guide and undergird a concerted Christian response to this crisis. At a time when many lament that theological dialogues are not bearing hoped-for fruit, it is worth noting, even celebrating, that the churches have begun to articulate and act on a shared theology of creation. More commitment is necessary, however, and the need is urgent and profoundly theological. Wes

---

1. *Global Environmental Outlook* [GEO 4, 2007]: *Summary for Decision Makers,* p. 4, at http://www.unep.org/geo/geo4/media/GEO4%20SDM_launch.pdf.

Granberg-Michaelson, who has done much to raise ecological awareness in the churches, puts it this way: "Rather than simply acknowledging immediate environmental problems that need remedy, our task is confronting the basic modern mind-set that spawns and rationalizes environmental ruin. This requires nothing short of the power of the gospel."[2]

In the Beginning . . .

It may now seem hard to believe, but the first speech to focus on a theology of creation at any major ecumenical gathering was an address by the American Lutheran theologian Joseph Sittler at the WCC's third assembly in 1961. "Is it again possible," asked Sittler, "to fashion a theology catholic enough to affirm redemption's force enfolding nature, as we have affirmed redemption's force enfolding history? That we should make that effort is, in my understanding, the commanding task of this moment" — a decidedly prescient observation, one year before publication of Rachel Carson's watershed book *Silent Spring,* about the devastating effects of pesticides and insecticides on the environment.

Human beings, said Sittler in his wonderful style, "blasphemously strut about this hurt and threatened world as if they owned it. . . . When atoms are disposable to the ultimate hurt, then the very atoms must be reclaimed for God and his will."[3] The radical character of Sittler's presentation becomes clear in light of the assembly's final report, which, typical of the age, says that "the Christian should welcome scientific discoveries as new steps in man's domination of nature."[4]

Why didn't the global ecumenical movement pay attention to environmental concerns prior to the 1960s? For the same two reasons the churches didn't: (1) The ideology of the Enlightenment emphasized the effort to subdue the natural world, to use it for human advancement. God's creation became "nature," a source of raw materials that were given value through

2. Wesley Granberg-Michaelson, "Covenant and Creation," at http://www.religion-online .org/showarticle.asp?title=2318.

3. Joseph Sittler, "Called to Unity," in Michael Kinnamon and Brian E. Cope, eds., *The Ecumenical Movement: An Anthology of Key Texts and Voices* (Grand Rapids: Eerdmans, 1997), pp. 288-289.

4. Quoted in David G. Hallman, "Climate Change: Ethics, Justice, and Sustainable Community," in Dieter T. Hessel and Rosemary Radford Ruether, eds., *Christianity and Ecology* (Cambridge: Harvard, 2000), p. 460.

exploitation. Such things as pollution, a deadly menace in European cities since the nineteenth century, were regarded as the inevitable, if sometimes regrettable, by-products of human progress. (2) The theological tradition in the West focused on God's redemptive activity in *human* history. Creation was taken as a preliminary to the gospel story. Nature was viewed as the "scenery" (Emil Brunner) before which the human drama played out, not as itself an object of God's work of salvation. This was Sittler's point. We have had, in his words, a Christology of the moral soul and a Christology of history, but not "a daring, penetrating, life-affirming Christology of nature."[5] And, thus, he took as his text the cosmic Christology of Colossians 1:15-20: "For by him were *all* things created. . . ."

It is instructive to note that the Orthodox churches have not, for the most part, been shaped by the western Enlightenment, and their theological tradition is much more insistently trinitarian. Whereas Protestant confessions usually begin with the second article of the creed, God's redemptive action in Christ, Orthodox theology begins with the first: God, Creator of heaven and earth. As a result, while many at the assembly in 1961 were reportedly puzzled by Sittler's presentation, the Orthodox were decidedly enthusiastic.

Sittler's speech gave impetus to a World Council of Churches (WCC) Faith and Order study on "Creation, New Creation, and the Unity of the Church," as well as the Faith-Man-Nature Group, supported by the National Council of Churches in the United States (NCC). These, however, were the exceptions in the ecumenical movement of the 1960s. The dominant theme of this period was human revolution, most notably expressed at the seminal conference on Church and Society, held in Geneva in 1966. The Geneva conference continued to speak of the human "mastery" of nature; and its final report even contended that "the physical world . . . does not have meaning in itself."[6]

The real wake-up call didn't come until the Club of Rome, a global think tank, issued its famous report on the "Limits to Growth" in 1972, its conclusion that earth cannot support the current pace of industrial development underscored by the oil embargo that rocked Europe and North America the following year. In response, the WCC began to emphasize the importance of "sustainability" — the idea that humans have a responsibility for the long-term impact of their policies and lifestyles, including (perhaps especially)

5. Sittler, "Called to Unity," p. 289.
6. *World Conference on Church and Society* (Geneva: WCC, 1967), pp. 196-98.

impact on the environment. It was a significant step when the council's fifth assembly (Nairobi, 1975) launched a study program, "Towards a Just, Participatory, and Sustainable Society," although the focus was still clearly anthropocentric. The next world conference on Church and Society, held at MIT in 1979, gave primary attention to science and new technology and their implications for human flourishing; but along with that came a growing concern for the ecological responsibility of the church.

This is not to say, however, that the concern was universally shared or commonly understood. At the WCC's sixth assembly in Vancouver (1983), great tension arose over ecumenical priorities, often experienced as justice versus ecology. I was on the World Council staff at the time of the Vancouver Assembly and vividly remember the response of persons from impoverished countries to the northern call for protection of the environment. It went something like this: "Now that you've cut down your forests and exploited our resources in order to build up your industrial base, you want us to be ecologically responsible?! Clean up your own mess! Our greatest need is economic growth for our people."

This debate helped generate a new WCC study program, this one called "Justice, Peace, and the Integrity of Creation" (JPIC), which sought to integrate these themes more fully and to inaugurate a process of covenant making between groups or churches struggling to realize different priorities in different contexts. The term "integrity of creation" was meant to signal that nature/creation has a value, an integrity, that comes from its origin in God, not simply a utility in the fulfillment of human aspirations. JPIC consultations rejected the language of "mastery" over creation and redefined "stewardship" in terms of solidarity with all creatures for whom the steward is responsible. The study culminated in a global convocation in Seoul (1990), where delegates offered ten shared affirmations, including one which affirms that creation is beloved of God: "Because creation is of God and the goodness of God permeates all creation, we hold all life to be sacred. . . . We will resist the claim that anything in creation is merely a resource for human exploitation."[7]

Since that time, the initiatives have proliferated beyond easy recounting. One priority for the WCC and its member churches has been to ensure ecumenical Christian presence at major international gatherings on the environment, such as the 1993 Earth Summit in Rio de Janeiro. Significant

---

7. "Ten Affirmations on Justice, Peace and the Integrity of Creation," in Kinnamon and Cope, eds., *The Ecumenical Movement*, pp. 321-22.

leadership in this period has been provided by the Orthodox churches. In 1989, the Ecumenical Patriarch Dimitrios I issued a patriarchal message calling for thanksgiving and supplications for all creation to be offered every September 1, the first day of the Orthodox ecclesiastical year. And his successor, Bartholomew, has been labeled the "Green Patriarch" because of his ecological activism. His insistence that destruction of the environment is not just folly but *sin* has marked an important step in Christian environmentalism.[8]

The NCC in the United States has had a highly effective and respected Ecojustice Working Group since 1984; but its work received a significant boost with the formation of the National Religious Partnership for the Environment in 1993. This funding coalition links the NCC with Catholic, Jewish, and evangelical Protestant partners, helping to raise substantial revenue for all of them. The working group, generally speaking, has focused on education as a way of integrating ecojustice into congregational life and providing a basis for public policy advocacy.

What We Now Agree On

As I survey the past half century of ecumenical thinking about creation/nature and the need for action to preserve it, it seems to me that the churches have commonly affirmed the following five principles or themes. These may seem fairly obvious to readers immersed in ecological ministry, but then shared affirmations often do. That itself is a sign of how deeply ecological ideas have penetrated the churches' consciousness, and another example of theological convergence achieved through ecumenical engagement.

1. The first principle is summarized in Psalm 24: *"The earth is the Lord's and all that is in it"* (v. 1). My favorite passage regarding "Jubilee," a biblical motif that connects economic and ecological justice, is Leviticus 25:23: "The land shall not be sold in perpetuity, for the land is mine [says the Lord]; with me you are but aliens and tenants" — or, as one colleague translates it, "with me you are but squatters." Since nature has its source in God and is provided as a gift of grace, it has intrinsic worth, is to be treated with respect, and should never be taken for granted. An "Open Letter," produced by the NCC's Ecojustice Working Group in 2005, declares

8. A number of the Patriarch's addresses on the environment can be found at www .patriarchate.org/environment.

that "the created world is sacred — a revelation of God's saving power and gracious presence filling all things."[9] This affirmation is a counter to those who forget the first article of the creed and jump straight to human redemption in Christ.

2. *Humans are an integral, relational part of nature.* As one strand in what some ecumenical documents refer to as the "web of life," we human beings have a divinely mandated responsibility to sustain the Earth, not dominate it for our own purposes. To put it another way, humans are created for communion with God, with one another, *and* with creation. There is, said Metropolitan John Zizioulas at the Fifth World Conference on Faith and Order (1993), "an intrinsic *koinonia* between human being and its natural environment"[10] — a conviction which makes clear that ecojustice is not simply an addendum to the agenda of the ecumenical movement. This affirmation counters the anthropocentric assumptions that have been so much a part of modern culture and western theology, including the assumption that humans are the sole bearers of moral value.

3. *Social justice and ecological justice are indivisible aspects of the church's mission.* Or, as Patriarch Bartholomew puts it, "Caring for the poor and caring for the Earth . . . are two sides of the same coin."[11] The following paragraph from a WCC study document on "Christian Faith and the World Economy Today" is illustrative:

> Poor people suffer disproportionately from environmental degradation. Often they live close to polluted areas, in inadequate housing conditions with poor sanitation. As peasants, they often only have access to poor, degraded and arid land. As landless agricultural workers, they are often exposed to toxic pesticides, insecticides, and herbicides. Often they see their drinking and fishing waters polluted and their health directly endangered.[12]

9. See "God's Earth Is Sacred: An Open Letter to Church and Society in the United States" at http://www.ncccusa.org/news/14.02.05theologicalstatement.html.

10. John Zizioulas (Metropolitan John of Pergamon), "The Church as Communion," in Thomas F. Best and Günter Gassmann, eds., *On the Way to Fuller Koinonia* (Geneva: WCC, 1994), p. 109.

11. Patriarch Bartholomew, "The Orthodox Church and the Environmental Crisis," in Lyndsay Moseley, ed., *Holy Ground: A Gathering of Voices on Caring for Creation* (San Francisco: Sierra Club Books, 2008), p. 40.

12. *Christian Faith and the World Economy Today: A Study Document from the World Council of Churches* (Geneva: WCC, 1992), p. 23.

Already in the early 1990s, the Ecojustice Working Group called attention to "environmental racism" — corporate decisions that target poor, usually minority, communities and government policies that provide unequal protection against toxic waste. African American church leaders who insist that their mission priority must be racism should, for that very reason, care deeply about matters of ecology. This affirmation is a counter to those who would split the ecumenical agenda, playing social justice and environmental protection off against one another.

4. *Since the human family is interdependent, and more truly so now in this age of globalization, decisions made about the environment in one part of the world, or patterns of acquisition and consumption practiced by one part of humanity, have enormous implications for those in other places or other economic strata.* Climate change, to take that example, is most assuredly an ethical issue, since it is largely precipitated by the overconsumption of fossil fuels in rich industrialized nations, while its consequences are experienced disproportionately by poor countries and island states.

A special responsibility falls to Christians and their churches in the United States, where 5 percent of the planet's population produces nearly one-fifth of the world's emissions and consumes a quarter of its natural resources. The NCC's "Open Letter" tries to state the challenge this poses in positive terms: "On a finite planet, frugality [a lifestyle of simplicity and conservation] is an expression of love and an instrument for justice and sustainability; it enables all life to thrive together by sparing and sharing global goods."[13] This principle has the effect of encouraging members of the body of Christ to recognize our ecological responsibility for people we will likely never meet.

5. *Christians live in hope (active expectation) of creation's fulfillment.* The Christian tradition does include an apocalyptic strand that envisions this world destroyed as a prelude to a new heaven and a new earth; but the ecumenical movement, certainly in recent years, has lifted up another strand of the biblical tradition, one that is expressed, for example, in the vision of the prophet Isaiah: "The desert shall rejoice and blossom as the rose. . . . The parched ground shall become a pool, and the thirsty land springs of water" (Isa. 35:1, 7, NKJV). This, of course, takes us back to Joseph Sittler and his call for "a theology catholic enough to affirm redemption's force enfolding nature" — although subsequent ecumenists have emphasized humanity's participation in the redemptive mission of God. This principle has the ef-

13. "God's Earth Is Sacred."

fect of encouraging us to recognize our ecological responsibility for future generations.

I probably should add a sixth affirmation, although it has been affirmed more as a matter of practice than of theology: The current assault on creation demands a collaborative response from all people of faith. We have been talking about the importance of ecumenical cooperation, but even that is too limited when it comes to protection of the environment. The global nature of an issue such as climate change, writes philosopher/environmentalist Roger Gottlieb, provides unparalleled motivation for *interfaith* engagement. "If there were ever an issue that clearly reveals the commonalities of human beings, despite differences in religious belief, ideology, or culture, this is the one."[14]

No Excuses

Ecumenism, as I hope this book demonstrates, has a broad agenda! No one can be fully involved in all parts of it. For much of my own ministry, I have not been an environmental activist — not because I haven't believed in its importance, but because my energy has been spent elsewhere. In recent years, however, I have begun to see that such things as poverty and war are inseparable from care for creation, and that even dialogues dealing with the theological intricacies of baptism or eucharist inevitably touch on the natural world. Beyond that, I now see that the ecological crisis of our era casts a shadow over everything else on the ecumenical agenda. So, perhaps, this chapter can be read as evidence of a personal "conversion," a personal call to activism, one that invites others to the same journey.

At the same time, I continue to wrestle with the literature summarized above. For example, while it is surely true that all creation expresses, in some measure, God's loving purpose, nature/creation seems more ambiguous, less idealized, than ecumenical documents sometimes let on. The moral theologian Ronald Preston, a loyal critic of the ecumenical movement, makes this point by quoting a friend's rewriting of the hymn "All Things Bright and Beautiful":

The darkness-loving cockroach,
the rat that carries fleas,

14. Roger S. Gottlieb, *A Greener Faith: Religious Environmentalism and Our Planet's Future* (Oxford: Oxford University Press, 2006), p. 126.

mosquito, louse, bacilli,
all bearers of disease.

The tsetse killing cattle,
the vampire sucking blood,
the Lord God all created
and saw that they were good.

The hairy-legged spider
that eats alive her mate,
the fly that tastes the dung hill
then vomits on your plate.

All things gross and dangerous,
all creatures great and small,
all things vile and murderous,
the Lord God made them all.[15]

The real point to be made is this: While humans have exploited nature in idolatrous ways that threaten its sustainability, it does not follow, as some texts appear to suggest, that humans should refrain from interfering in nature for the sake of improving human life. Some ecumenical statements sound as if nature were "fixed," static. But isn't it more the case that nature is always in flux? And don't humans have a proper role in such evolution? Human creativity, as I see it, is a gift that is appropriately used on behalf of human purposes. If I could authorize the eradication of malaria-carrying mosquitoes, I would do so in a heartbeat! The challenge is to do so in a way that promotes a sustainable environment — and that is where the hard conversation begins.

To come at this another way, Scripture does depict humans as part of the natural order, but also as holding a distinctive place of honor and responsibility in it. "A little lower than the angels" is how the psalmist puts it (Psalm 8:5). When push comes to shove, if it is a choice between providing safe water for humans and preserving the habitat of an endangered frog. . . . As Granberg-Michaelson observes, "in specific contexts, it often seems that choices are demanded between ecology and economic justice — between

15. Ronald Preston, "Humanity, Nature and the Integrity of Creation," *Ecumenical Review* 41: 558.

preserving trees or cooking food."[16] But the complexity of the questions should in no way be an excuse for avoiding action. It is simply a further invitation to join this ecumenical, action-oriented conversation.

16. Wesley Granberg-Michaelson, "Towards a Theology of Life," *Reformed World* 44 (September 1994).

CHAPTER 6

Can the Tension Between Unity and Justice Be Overcome?

It is an increasingly familiar conversation. The pastor of a downtown church, known for its progressive witness, speaks to me with animation about the number of Hispanic members who are joining the congregation. These new members bring a lively approach to worship, great food to the potluck dinners, and their own justice priorities, especially immigration reform. It all feels, says the pastor, like an answer to our prayer that the congregation will become more diverse — less like a culturally homogeneous social club and more like the global body of Christ! But, her voice drops, it has also been harder than she imagined, because these new members also bring a conservative theological background that threatens to weaken the congregation's historic commitment to such things as environmental protection, reduced military spending, and gay rights (which is an absolutely crucial justice issue for many of the white members). She is able to preach about racial justice, which has become low-hanging fruit; but when she ventures into other areas, it shakes the tenuous unity of the congregation.

The president of a local council of churches recounts how, some years ago, he quit a job rather than participate in discrimination against the LGBT community. Now, however, he is getting flak from some members of the council's board after he discouraged them from presenting a resolution supporting the state's referendum to legalize same-sex marriage. How could we take such a stand, he asks (with obvious pain), when our members include black, Orthodox, and Catholic parishes that strongly oppose the marriage referendum for what they argue are theological reasons? Sure, a resolution might pass, but at what cost to the fellowship of the council?

Increasing Tension

The perennial tension between unity and justice — which, as these conversations remind us, is played out in congregations as well as denominations and ecumenical organizations — is growing more acute in our era for two quite obvious reasons: (1) The voices of marginalized and oppressed groups have, thankfully, grown more insistent, harder to ignore — in society and in the church, in the United States and around the world. Within the ecumenical movement, a concern for justice now dominates the agenda in many settings. (2) At the same time, there is a growing appreciation for the diversity of human community, which inevitably includes not only racial, ethnic, and cultural differences, but those of theology and ideology as well. The ecumenical movement, which (despite repeated statements that unity is not uniformity) once saw diversity as a problem to be overcome, now generally affirms that genuine diversity is constitutive of the unity we seek. And thus the tension: the broader the table, the narrower the set of justice issues that can be commonly addressed. The more passionate a community is about either unity-in-diversity or justice, the harder it is to hold them together.

Examples of this tension abound. I have had the privilege of teaching in seminaries in India where a high percentage of students come from a Dalit (formerly called "untouchable") background. As the visiting professor of ecumenical studies, I would emphasize that "Christian" is the noun that unites us. We are Protestant *Christians* and Catholic *Christians,* related at a level deeper than church tradition. We are Indian Christians and American Christians, related at a level deeper than nationality. We are liberal Christians and conservative Christians, related at a level deeper than political ideology. We are Dalit Christians and "upper caste" Christians, related. . . . At this point, they would object: "Yes, these others are part of the church; but when it comes to 'unity,' our deepest bonds are with other Dalits, not with Christians who may not truly join the struggle against caste oppression." There is a limit to the diversity they can affirm.

In the United States, we see such an extensive split between those whose priority is justice and those whose priority is church unity that it is often difficult to speak of one ecumenical movement. Every March about eight hundred Christians from various denominations gather in the Washington, D.C., area for Ecumenical Advocacy Days, the aim of which is to offer common witness on current social-political issues. Most of the participants, if I am not mistaken, think of unity primarily as inter-denominational collaboration and are interested in such unity to the extent that it contributes to peace, justice, and care for creation. Then in April, three hundred or so Christians attend the National Workshops on Christian Unity, with a stated goal of promoting visible communion — rooted in the church's apostolic heritage and centered in the eucharist — with a methodology of painstaking theological dialogue. Both groups would say that they are central to ecumenism in the U.S.; and, in my experience, there is almost no overlap between them.

The report from the 1983 assembly of the World Council of Churches (WCC) states the matter clearly and succinctly:

> For some, the search for a unity in one faith and one eucharistic fellowship seems, at best secondary, at worst irrelevant to the struggles for peace, justice, and human dignity; for others, the church's political involvement against the evils of history seems, at best secondary, at worst detrimental to its role as Eucharistic community and witness to the gospel.[1]

Nearly all denominations and ecumenical bodies institutionalize this bifurcation by assigning justice and unity to separate departments, thus setting up a competition for resources and influence.

Constructive Convictions

My own position is probably evident from the way I frame the issue. In my judgment, the ecumenical vision of the church is impoverished not by those who start with, even emphasize, either justice or unity, but by those who divide the agenda, playing one off against the other. This is a movement that, at its best, speaks of *Baptism, Eucharist, and Ministry* and "Programme to Combat Racism," "Joint Declaration on Justification" and "Decade to Overcome Violence," in the same breath. As I have indicated, holding the tension between unity and justice is not easy, but the attempt to do so is precisely when the ecumenical vision becomes most profound and the ecumenical movement most vital.

The relationship of unity and justice has been the focus of several major studies, especially in the context of the WCC. Out of these studies have come at least six convictions that I hope can be commonly affirmed. The first two may seem fairly obvious (although hard won!); the latter four will take more

---

1. David Gill, ed., *Gathered for Life: Official Report of the Sixth Assembly of the World Council of Churches* (Geneva: WCC, 1983), p. 49.

explanation. Taken together, these affirmations do not resolve the tension between justice and unity, but they do, as I see it, help us to address it more constructively:

1. *The evils that divide human society — racism, sexism, great economic disparity, violence — also divide the church.* Racism, for example, is not only a question of social justice but of ecclesiology. It is a radical distortion of the Christian faith (which affirms that *all* humans are created in the image of God) and of the church that proclaims it; and it has divided the followers of Christ every bit as much as, if not more than, different theologies of the sacraments or different understandings of justification.

As obvious as this may sound, Christians should not take it for granted. A case in point is the Consultation on Church Union (COCU), an American church unity effort now known as Churches Uniting in Christ, that includes three predominately African American denominations. Until 1980, COCU's theological consensus document referred to racism and sexism only in an appendix. The real "theological issues," it was assumed, were such things as sacraments, teaching authority, ministry, and creeds. The others were "social issues" that have what COCU documents called "church-dividing potential."[2] This division of the agenda continues, at least implicitly, in many of the bilateral dialogues.

2. *Unity and justice actually help define one another.* On the one hand, the search for unity can bolster ingrained forms of domination unless intentionally coupled with a commitment to just relationships. Letty Russell, a theologian well known in both feminist and ecumenical circles, put it this way: "[A] crucial criterion for the authenticity of any unity proposal is whether it contributes to the wholeness and well-being of marginalized people."[3] On the other hand, the justice we seek is not merely the co-existence of separated communities, but a new community in which walls of hostility have come down, one in which those who have been excluded have a place. A united church should be a witness for justice not only through its external commitments, but through the way its diverse members live with one another.

3. *Unity, like grace, is a gift that demands a costly response.* Just as Dietrich Bonhoeffer warned against "cheap grace," so ecumenists should warn against a "cheap unity" that avoids contentious issues because they can be disruptive.

---

2. *In Quest of a Church of Christ Uniting,* Revised 1980 (Princeton, N.J.: Consultation on Church Union, 1980). See, especially, Appendix B.

3. Letty Russell, "Women and Unity: Problem or Possibility," *Midstream* 21 (July 1982): 298-304.

This was a major theme in a study on "Ecclesiology and Ethics," carried out by the WCC in the 1990s. "Costly unity," said the study participants, "is discovering the churches' unity as a gift of pursuing justice and peace."[4] Some U.S. churches, for example, found themselves internally divided by decisions to support the Civil Rights struggle or the anti-war protests of the 1960s (especially when these decisions involved civil disobedience), only to discover deeper unity with others through shared public witness. Costly unity means a refusal to withdraw from the ambiguities of historical action in order to preserve a shallow harmony in the church.

Twenty years earlier, the World Council's Faith and Order Commission produced a short statement on this theme — titled "Towards Unity in Tension" — that also warrants further study. The tone of the text is appropriately paradoxical: "An ecclesiastical unity which would stand in the way of struggles for liberation would be a repressive unity," and any unity that papers over fundamental differences with regard to justice and peace would be vacuous. At the same time,

> the church has also been given remarkable anticipations of [oneness in Christ], even in the midst of severe conflict. The church must, therefore, bear the tension of conflicts within itself, and so fulfill its ministry of reconciliation, in obedience to the Lord who chose to sacrifice himself rather than to confer on the forces of division any ultimate authority.[5]

This is costly unity: acknowledging the inevitable tension that goes with social advocacy, giving witness to our unity in Christ "even with those from whom we may, for his sake, have to part."[6]

4. As Tom Best, a longtime member of the Faith and Order staff, has observed, the assumption behind the previous point, and specifically the text "Towards Unity in Tension," is that *unity is not something which we have to create, but is a reality already given by God.*[7] A concern for justice may lead to strenuous disagreement with other churches or with other members of one's own church; but, in the final analysis, Christian communion is not

4. Thomas F. Best and Martin Robra, eds., *Ecclesiology and Ethics* (Geneva: WCC, 1997), p. 6.

5. "Towards Unity in Tension," in Michael Kinnamon and Brian E. Cope, eds., *The Ecumenical Movement: An Anthology of Key Texts and Voices* (Grand Rapids: Eerdmans, 1997), p. 109.

6. Kinnamon and Cope, eds., *The Ecumenical Movement*, p. 109.

7. Thomas F. Best, ed., *Beyond Unity-in-Tension* (Geneva: WCC, 1988), p. 31.

constituted by our agreement. It is a gift of the "God who was in Christ reconciling the world to himself" (2 Cor. 5:19). Indeed, this scriptural insight ought to free Christians to disagree — passionately! — without breaking fellowship.

I love the way that Elizabeth Templeton, a theologian from the Reformed Church in Scotland, puts it in her provocative collection of essays *The Strangeness of God:*

> The church must refuse to domesticate our exclusions as having a part in God's future. In this it challenges all the belongings which define us against one another. So help him God, Gerry Adams is called to banquet with Ian Paisley. [Or as Americans might say, William Sloane Coffin is called to banquet with Pat Robertson.] So help me God, I am called to banquet with both, and everything in my guts doesn't want to! I must, where I humanly belong, takes sides on issues involving both. Yet I am only allowed to take sides on the basis of a recognition that who I am in Christ in some sense has to take them in.[8]

Templeton is surely correct: There *are* times when Christians must take sides against others who claim the name of Christ. Even in such moments, however, our understanding of church must be shaped more by theology than politics. Even in such moments, we must recognize that the "them" we oppose are, in some fundamental way, "us." The ecumenical church cannot fear controversy or confrontation because such fear could paralyze a commitment to justice; but Christians must hate division because the story of our faith tells us that we have been linked in communion with persons we might otherwise shun. Nothing else can testify so powerfully that our trust is in God, not in communities of our own devising.[9]

5. Templeton's reference to God's future leads to the fifth point: *Unity is not only a gift to be embodied here and now; it is, as well, an eschatological goal — a part of God's promised reign toward which we are called.* Because unity is a gift, Christians should be prepared to stay at the table despite disagreement; but because unity is an eschatological calling,

---

8. Elizabeth Templeton, *The Strangeness of God* (London: Arthur James, 1993), p. 94.

9. Sometimes, in class, I will ask students whether their deepest source of communal identity is in groups of like-minded peace advocates or in the church with its hawks and doves. Ecumenical Christians, it seems to me, will answer (however reluctantly) "In the church," because it is there that we attempt to live out the gospel while living with those who hear in it a different mandate and who, thus, challenge our own self-righteousness.

Christians should also be prepared to disrupt our present, partial "unities" in order to manifest that deeper, wider unity of God's promise. What is church union, after all, but a disruption of present fellowship for the sake of greater wholeness?

This has lots of practical implications. I was on the staff of the WCC's Faith and Order Commission when the commission completed work on *Baptism, Eucharist, and Ministry* (BEM) and sent it to the churches for official response. And I recall several church leaders urging us not to pursue discussions about women in ministry since this would "rock the boat," would threaten the fragile accommodation on the subject arrived at in BEM. But ecumenists, of course, are in the boat-rocking business! Whatever you think about the ordination of women (and whether or not it is a justice issue), all such topics are fair game for discussion as we seek to grow more fully into the gift of oneness as the church.

At the WCC's Nairobi Assembly in 1975, the great Indian church leader M. M. Thomas argued that Christ shatters every unity that turns into idolatrous bondage and frees us to establish a more mature unity — only to shatter that, too, when it turns oppressive.[10] Without this understanding of church unity as present gift *and* eschatological promise (already and not yet), Christians will likely be unable to hold the tension I have been describing.

6. Since no ecumenical leader has articulated the integration of unity and justice more eloquently or persistently than M. M. Thomas, it seems appropriate to let him make the sixth point: *Acting for justice is usually more ambiguous than we acknowledge.* In one of his addresses as moderator of the WCC's Central Committee, Thomas raised the hardest of all ecumenical questions: Can there be unity as long as the church includes both oppressed and oppressors? The problem with this question, said Thomas,

> is that the lines are always more blurred than that. When compared to the West, I am a victim; when compared to the poor of India, I am a victimizer. Beyond that, the question overlooks the reality of divine forgiveness, which enables the oppressed to trust and the oppressor to repent, [and which] is always breaking in and transforming the conditions of our world.[11]

10. M. M. Thomas, *Towards a Theology of Contemporary Ecumenism* (Madras: CLS, 1978), p. 316.
11. Thomas, *Towards a Theology,* pp. 261-62.

To come at this from another angle, justice, like unity, is of God and not finally achieved by human endeavor. Our struggles for it should always be accompanied by a humility that recognizes the sinfulness even of uniters and liberators.

As a former general secretary of the National Council of Churches (NCC), I want to acknowledge that the NCC, probably like most councils, has not always adequately maintained this tension between unity and justice. The work of the National Council's Faith and Order Commission, the purpose of which is to promote visible church unity, has been regarded by some NCC leaders as an esoteric drag on, or diversion from, what they take to be the primary task: justice and advocacy. At the same time, controversial issues, such as human sexuality, are often avoided for fear of division, thus revealing a failure to grasp that unity is a gift and not a product of our agreement.

In my presentations to the Governing Board, I insisted that the NCC is *both* a diverse forum where conflicting perspectives meet in dialogue *and* a (somewhat unified) community that boldly declares the gospel's partisanship on behalf of the excluded and oppressed. If the NCC governing structures move too quickly on questions of poverty and peace, they risk leaving member churches behind or alienating them. If, however, they try to marshal the whole community, they risk missing the moment when the council's voice is needed.[12] The diversity of conciliar membership would be a liability if councils were purely utilitarian organizations — but that, of course, would miss the point. On the other hand, these communities of churches are also not debate societies — and dare not be in a world where so many are in such need.

In thinking about this, I am indebted to the work of Willem Visser 't Hooft, first general secretary of the WCC. "The World Council," he wrote in one of his later books, "has a special responsibility to maintain the fellowship between its member churches, for the achievement of this fellowship [with all its tensions] is the real *raison d'etre* of the World Council. . . . But," he adds, "it is a fellowship based on common convictions and called to common witness. An important element in the very substance of our fellowship is what we have hammered out together in our assemblies"[13] — including a common commitment to combat racism and sexism, to stand with the poor in their

---

12. See chapter 7.

13. W. A. Visser 't Hooft, *Has the Ecumenical Movement a Future?* (Belfast: Christian Journals Ltd., 1974), p. 43.

push for economic justice, to bear witness that war is contrary to the will of God, and to declare the preciousness of God's good creation.

It is important to say this carefully. Specific social-political commitments are not a prerequisite for ecumenical participation; but certain commitments *are* part of the fabric of witness now woven through the churches' life together as a result of their conciliar dialogue and their common submission to the gospel. To say it another way, those who know themselves bound together in Christ will try to express the mind of Christ in one faith, one ministry, one sacramental life, and *one obedience.* Shared ethical commitments are a significant and visible part of the council's deepening fellowship.

Just Say No

I will end by recalling an incident that occurred in 1991 — not in an ecumenical context, but during my nomination to become General Minister and President of my denomination, the Christian Church (Disciples of Christ). That nomination was ultimately defeated, primarily because of my support for the lesbian and gay community and their full participation in the church and its leadership; but, as part of the process, I spoke to gatherings of Disciples across the country, often in places where the opposition was most intense.[14] One of those meetings was in Cleveland. I gave introductory remarks and then opened the floor for questions and comments. The first man to speak (a Disciples minister, I was later told) started out rather blandly, and I was mentally drifting — vaguely anticipating where his observations might go — when suddenly I heard him say, "After all, these homosexuals are just worthless scum." There were lots of tough moments during the nomination, but this one haunted me more than any other because I was in the position of leadership and did not denounce him.

Why didn't I? I tried to tell myself I was just caught off guard, but the truth cuts deeper — and it has to do with the tension named in this chapter. My life's work as an ecumenist centers on reconciliation, on the attempt to hold community together, on the insistence that diverse voices be heard. But that evening I realized that there was something fundamentally impoverished about an understanding of reconciliation that left me unprepared to respond immediately and forcefully — in the name of God's justice — to this man.

14. For a reflection on this experience, see Michael Kinnamon, "Restoring Mainline Trust: Disagreeing in Love," *Christian Century* (July 1-8, 1992): 645-48.

My best dialogue partner for all this turned out to be the apostle Paul. Paul, it seems to me, could live with a unity of enormous diversity, as long as all parties recognized that they were the undeserving recipients of grace. But as soon as one party began to claim it had defined the boundaries of grace, then, for Paul, God's gracious "yes!" to the world became a resounding "no!" to human pretensions. "Welcome one another," he writes to the Roman church, "just as Christ has welcomed you, for the glory of God" (Rom. 15:7).[15] Such welcome is not tolerance; it is active embrace. And it demands, I came to realize, that we say no to those ways of acting and those ways of thinking that do not welcome others as Christ has welcomed us. This is paradoxical, but such paradox, I now believe, is at the heart of Christian faith.

The crucial insight of modern ecumenism is not that we should unite with Christians we find agreeable, but that God has bound us in communion with people we are not necessarily like and may not find likable. This is what gives the ecumenical movement its prophetic edge. U.S. Christians cannot say to Cuban Christians, "We have no need of you." White Christians cannot say to Christians of color, "We have no need of you." Though everything in my guts doesn't want to, I must recognize the man in Cleveland as my brother in Christ. But this relatedness, I see now, is precisely the point. For his sake and the church's, my response should have been, "Brother, sit down! Such talk has nothing to do with the Good News of gracious welcome we proclaim. Such talk has no place in a community of those who know they are redeemed only by grace."

Speaking out for justice. Affirming the unity of those who are different. This is the core of ecumenism. This is the challenge of the gospel.

---

15. The most focused treatment of this theme, in my judgment, is Paul's letter to the Galatians.

CHAPTER 7

Has the Ecumenical Movement
Become Too "Political"?

The criticism most often leveled at the ecumenical movement and its prominent expressions (e.g., the world and national councils of churches) is that they have become too "political." One of the most widely discussed of these attacks was an article published in 1993 in *Reader's Digest,* which slammed the World Council of Churches (WCC) for drifting from its original goal of Christian unity "into the choppy waters of 'secular ecumenism' — ministering to society through political activism."[1] In ecumenical circles, work for social transformation through political action is generally referred to as "advocacy" (the National Council of Churches [NCC], for example, has had a Justice and Advocacy Commission); so I want to begin this discussion by asking: Is political advocacy an appropriate dimension of Christian witness?

It is important to underscore that advocacy, at least in the U.S. context, is not a matter of endorsing candidates or political parties, which churches are not legally permitted to do, but of taking public stands on issues in order to influence public opinion and legislative or administrative decision making. Advocacy, as practiced by ecumenical councils, also should not be confused with "lobbying." Lobbying is political pressure brought to bear on behalf of those with resources. Advocacy is political pressure brought to bear on behalf of those with few resources — the poor, immigrants, the disabled, children, those who suffer from war and other forms of violence. Is this an appropriate dimension of Christian witness?

Many faithful and intelligent Christians would answer no. Political ad-

---

1. At http://www.pravoslavieto.com/docs/eng/gospel_accord_marx.htm.

vocacy, some of them argue, compromises the church's primary work, which has to do with a person's relationship with God — divine justice rather than social justice. (I recall one student who was cautious about advocacy because, if the churches are successful, "the credit will go to the government instead of to Christ," and our task is to glorify him.) Others point out that advocacy can be divisive, undermining the church's sense of community and threatening its essential unity. Individual Christians certainly make political decisions based on their understanding of the gospel, but when the church as a whole tries to do so, it inevitably alienates some members who believe their faith calls for a different course of action. Still others contend that the separation of church and state precludes the church's involvement in political controversy.

These are not isolated opinions. Studies cited in a widely referenced book from 2002, *The Quiet Hand of God: Faith-Based Activism and the Public Role of Mainline Protestantism*, found that 26 percent of pastors think it inappropriate for their denominations to take positions on political issues, and that "85 percent of church members participate in direct service ministries, while only 10 percent participate in advocacy."[2] My own denomination, faced with declining numbers and resources, has eliminated virtually all national staff positions responsible for social justice ministries, and leaders are trying to minimize, if not eliminate, General Assembly resolutions that deal with potentially divisive contemporary issues. As a result, advocacy is increasingly confined to special interest groups that can be ignored by the rest of the church.

Saying Yes to Advocacy

There are, of course, counterarguments that encourage Christian engagement in advocacy, ones that I find persuasive. It is often pointed out, for example, that lack of political engagement *is* political engagement in that it perpetuates the status quo and, thus, works against the most vulnerable members of society. Others emphasize that separation of church and state has never meant, cannot mean, the separation of faith from public life — for individuals or religious communities. If a community claims that Christ

2. Robert Wuthnow and John H. Evans, eds., *The Quiet Hand of God: Faith-Based Activism and the Public Role of Mainline Protestantism* (Berkeley: University of California Press, 2002), pp. 70 and 229.

is Lord of its life, that it is shaped by faith in God, how can it refrain from making its perspective known as one voice in the pluralistic public dialogue?

Scripture was written in political contexts so different from our own that it is hard to appeal to it as precedent. Nonetheless, it is worth noting that the Bible speaks of God's preoccupation with how communities organize their common life and allocate their resources (i.e., the stuff of politics) — with true weights and measures in the marketplace; with the honesty of judges; with hospitality to strangers; with the plight of the poor, the widow, and the orphan; with turning swords into plowshares. Isaiah, typical of the Bible's prophetic strand, rails against those "who make iniquitous decrees, who write oppressive statutes, to turn aside the needy from justice and to rob the poor of my people of their right" (Isa. 10:1-2).[3]

To put it more theologically, the Christian doctrines of creation and incarnation affirm that life in *this* world, though distorted by sin, is supremely precious to God. The church's role is not simply to focus on "spiritual things" or the "hereafter," but to be a credible sign and instrument of social transformation toward the day when God's will for shalom is realized on earth as it is in heaven.

With those things in mind, ecumenically engaged churches have generally agreed that advocacy is an appropriate, even essential, dimension of Christian mission. Obviously, it is possible to overemphasize advocacy — at the expense of such things as education, evangelism, and worship — or to fail to ground it theologically in the church's proclamation. I am convinced, however, that common witness to Christ, theological dialogue aimed at unity in the body of Christ, and advocacy for justice and peace in Christ's name are complementary responses to the gospel and should, therefore, be regarded as inseparable parts of the ecumenical vision of the church.

The biggest question for me is how to carry out advocacy effectively in an ecumenical context. I suspect it is always easier to do advocacy work through a coalition approach, which seeks common cause with like-minded partners, than through a conciliar approach, which seeks consensus within a community of divergent perspectives. Being part of an ecumenical community demands that we be concerned with the priority issues of others, that their perspectives be taken fully into account. Needless to say, this complicates the already difficult task of advocacy.

My own experience — as chairperson of the NCC's Justice and Advo-

---

3. A good summary of the biblical call to advocacy can be found in the annual *Public Policy Briefing Book* of the United Church of Christ, available online.

cacy Commission and, later, as the council's general secretary — has convinced me that advocacy undertaken by ecumenical bodies is most effective and profound when it wrestles with seven tensions. This is not a checklist of things to do, but of things to keep in mind. It is not meant as a blueprint for successful advocacy (as if that were possible!), but as a distillation of what one person has learned from the effort.

Seven Tensions

1. The first tension that must be named is the need for the social witness of councils of churches to reflect the will of their members, while also prophetically challenging the churches to live out the full calling of the gospel. Church representatives on the boards of councils are notorious for voting to take pioneering advocacy positions that their own churches are not yet ready to take (a dynamic that is also true of denominational assemblies and their relationship with congregations). Sometimes this brings positive results — for example, early conciliar opposition to the 2003 war in Iraq seemed to prod several churches to make their own stand on behalf of peace. But, of course, a council speaks with authority to the wider society only when people in the pews, not just their leaders, say "Amen." I know from painful experience that the NCC is too often perceived as generals without an army, as a thirty-eighth entity rather than a community of thirty-seven churches that collectively represent forty-five million believers.

This, like all tensions, must be expressed carefully. Councils of churches are *both* instruments of the churches *and* of the ecumenical movement. As José Miguez Bonino once said of the WCC, the council is both a "space" where different ecclesial partners gather to celebrate, discuss, and cooperate and an avant-garde movement that challenges the churches through pioneering action and risky theological formulation.[4] As general secretary of the NCC, I did not see it as my job to press an advocacy agenda on the members; but it was precisely my job to push them to enact the implications of decisions they made together. If the churches have declared in ecumenical assembly that "war is contrary to the will of God,"[5] then ecumenical leaders should insist on asking, "What does this mean for us and our country here

4. José Miguez Bonino, "The Concern for a Vital and Coherent Theology," *Ecumenical Review* 41 (April 1989): 172.
5. See chapter 3.

and now?" To put it another way, the fellowship experienced in an ecumenical community is rooted not only in what the churches *are*, but in what they are called to *become*. Only with this in mind can we sustain the paradox of both working through the churches and being ahead of them.

2. I want to get at the second tension by pointing to a book that did not receive the attention it deserved when published in 2006: *Beyond Idealism: A Way Ahead for Ecumenical Social Ethics*. In it, the authors — who include such respected scholars as Julio de Santa Ana, Heidi Hadsell, and Lewis Mudge — argue for a perspective they call "hopeful realism," a realistic assessment of our social situation coupled with a willingness to imagine and proclaim alternative realities.[6] On the one hand, ecumenical councils have often responded to war or discrimination or environmental destruction with idealized slogans and utopian pronouncements. On the other hand, the NCC, to take the example I know best, has often been reactive to the world's agenda, promoting reforms that, while important, leave the underlying status quo basically untouched.

A good example of this tension came during the days I was putting this chapter in final form. Several clergy colleagues from Seattle-area churches gathered with interfaith friends for a press conference to announce our support for legislation banning assault weapons and high-capacity ammunition magazines (used in a recent mass shooting of children) and closing background-check loopholes for people purchasing guns. This carefully focused agenda was undercut, however, by one speaker who launched an attack on the Second Amendment and gun ownership in general, thereby giving "ammunition" to the National Rifle Association and its allies.

As I see it, ecumenical leaders cannot stop pushing for raises in the minimum wage or calling for more recycling or urging a reduction in military spending or, as in this case, promoting a limited agenda to reduce gun violence. These are realistic steps that have some promise of success. But, as our colleague in Seattle apparently knew, these are but ways of tweaking systems, and, thus, they stop short of a truly prophetic witness that engenders hope for a different way of living in human society.

One person who argues this case is Gary Dorrien, Reinhold Niebuhr Professor of Social Ethics at Union Theological Seminary. Without a social vision of the Good Society that transcends the prevailing order, Dorrien contends, Christian ethics will remain captive to that order, and socially engaged

---

6. Julio de Santa Ana et al., *Beyond Idealism: A Way Ahead for Ecumenical Social Ethics* (Grand Rapids: Eerdmans, 2006). See, especially, pp. ix-xxv.

Christianity will restrict itself to marginal reforms.[7] I am also persuaded by the way that Audrey Chapman, former executive of the United Church of Christ Board for World Ministries, puts it: "Our churches seem limited to recommending incremental policy changes that differ little from secular political actions." What is often missing, in her words, "is a compelling religious vision, a sense of the 'now' and the 'not yet' of God's Kingdom that challenges and opposes the injustices of the dominant reality by invoking God's peace and justice."[8]

Remember Dr. King's great refrain "I have a dream" — of the day when black children and white children play together, when the empty stomachs of Mississippi are filled. This is not wishful thinking. It is imagining the world as our gracious God would have it. And, as such, it helps set our larger agenda.

Hopeful realism. *We* cannot eradicate evil. The conceit of such utopianism has itself been the fuel of countless tyrannies; and a focus on the perfect can indeed be the enemy of getting good things done. But we also dare not allow those responsible for present systems of injustice to define what is possible, because we are followers of One whose promise is not just for another world but for this world made other.

3. The third tension will be clear to any student of American churches. Ecumenical Christianity, which once was a highly influential player in U.S. political life, is now but one, by no means dominant, voice in the public discussion of contemporary issues. This calls for greater humility than the churches may have shown in the past, even as they dare not lose the confidence (humble confidence) that comes from their efforts to reflect the will of God for human community.

In 1951, one year after its founding, the NCC adopted a policy statement on the churches' "corporate influence in the nation and the world." The statement exudes assurance that the churches, acting as council, would be taken seriously by the society, that the council's advocacy could help shape the course of public debate on matters demanding legislative and judicial attention.

Much has changed since 1951! Mainline Protestant denominations, which for decades have been the pillars of conciliar ecumenism, have lost not

7. Gary Dorrien, *Soul in Society: The Making and Renewal of Social Christianity* (Minneapolis: Fortress, 1995), p. 344.

8. Audrey R. Chapman, *Faith, Power, and Politics: Political Ministry in the Mainline Churches* (New York: Pilgrim Press, 1991), p. 88.

only members but their culturally favored position. Evangelical and Catholic leaders are now more often quoted in the media than those from ecumenical Protestant communions, and the statements of the NCC are simply one part of a multi-religious witness.

Yet, while the churches that together constitute the NCC surely had more worldly power in 1951 than they do today, it is questionable whether they had more "authority," at least as authority is understood in Scripture. Many ecumenically engaged Christians will lament the loss of such power, but it should not be confused with the more fundamental issue of the church's authority in the world. An NCC policy statement from 2010 has the theology right:

> The authority of the church in the world is not an authority of worldly power, but one that reveals in holiness and truth the love of God through faithful acts of healing and forgiveness and reconciliation. . . . The church's authority is rooted in its identity as the People of God, the Body of Christ, the New Creation of the Holy Spirit — a community of human beings called to embody and enact the graciousness it has received.[9]

So, yes, there is reason for humility, including contrition for the ways we have been not only *in* the world but too much *of* it, coveting power. But there is also reason to give thanks for the ministry God has done and continues to do in and through us — and to declare this work of God boldly.

4. The fourth tension could have been added to either of the previous two, although I think it is worth making it a separate point (if only briefly): the need to work with political leaders and government officials in order to get things accomplished and the equally pressing need to avoid being co-opted by them. It is always a danger, for example, that leaders in the NCC will temper criticism of a President's actions or lack of action in order to ensure access to the White House. If such access becomes an end in itself (the allure of rubbing shoulders with the politically powerful), then an ecumenical body has undercut its credibility and trampled on its message. If, however, such access is seen as a tool for promoting the cause of peace or concern for the poor, then who can deny its value? A difficult tension!

5. Another not-unrelated tension is the need, on the one hand, for focused attention to particular advocacy priorities, and the need, on the

---

9. "The Authority of the Church in the World," at http://www.ncccusa.org/pdfs/authority ofthechurch.pdf.

other, for advocacy that integrates multiple themes, that sees our particular and immediate problems in wider context. As general secretary, I spent a good deal of time arguing, in line with NCC policy, that quality public education for all is a justice issue. But, of course, we cannot simply focus on education alone, since a large part of the problem is inequitable funding based on patterns of race and class. Public education needs priority attention, even as it cannot be dealt with as an isolated concern. Similarly, the NCC's Governing Board appropriately insisted that "a just rebuilding of the Gulf Coast" in the aftermath of Hurricane Katrina demanded recognition that poverty, racism, and environmental devastation form a "web of oppression," each issue inseparable from the others. Yet the council's assembly also rightly affirmed that, while such an integrated approach is vital, it is not sufficient. Racism, for example, demands specific focus, lest it be subsumed under another agenda and treated as less pressing than in previous generations.

As general secretary, I quickly came to appreciate the need to be *very* specific if my advocacy efforts were to bear fruit. For example, in repeated conversations with Jewish colleagues, including the Israeli ambassador to the United States, I stressed three deep concerns related to the Israeli-Palestinian conflict — the revocation of the residence permits of Jerusalemites who study or work abroad, the separation of Palestinian families when a husband and wife have different residence permits or one is an Israeli citizen, and the delay in approving building permits in Palestinian areas — because on these I saw some possibility of positive outcome. If this were all the National Council did or said, however, it would mask the even deeper issue of Israeli occupation of Palestinian land, with all the suffering and injustice that has entailed. Both focused attention *and* attention to the broader picture are needed. At the end of the day, I must admit that much of our advocacy work at the NCC fell somewhere in-between: not specific enough to get as much done as we would like, and not broad enough to see specific issues in wider perspective.

A related dilemma is that the NCC — like other councils, I fear — has often dissipated its energy and resources on an almost endless list of causes (running the danger of what a former leader of the British Council of Churches called "omnipotent mediocrity"[10]), in part because its members have different priorities. For immigrant churches with roots in the Middle East, it may be the persecution of Christians and their emigration from the

---

10. See Lesslie Newbigin, *A Word in Season* (Grand Rapids: Eerdmans, 1994), p. 193.

region. For historic peace churches, it may be selective conscientious objection as a challenge to the culture of militarism. For the black churches, it may be the disparity in sentencing for possession of crack or powder cocaine. How can a council take seriously the priorities of very diverse members and, at the same time, stay focused on overriding issues of the day?

6. That question leads to a sixth tension: the need to respond with appropriate urgency to crises of the moment and the equally urgent need for long-term formation so that advocacy grows from the churches' very identity. In the U.S., in my experience, churches seem to discover issues with an evangelical zeal (e.g., gun control in the aftermath of a mass killing), but often retain only a short-term commitment because they are missing long-term formation.

Again, Chapman makes the case powerfully in her book *Faith, Power, and Politics*. "In the absence of shared understandings about identity and vocation," she writes,

> . . . political ministry tends to be unfocused and diffuse, lacking explicit theological grounding and sustained membership support and involvement. Political witness tends to become a specialized mission activity undertaken primarily by national agencies . . . on behalf of the denominations, rather than an expression of the community's faith journey.[11]

And this leads to a familiar form of hypocrisy whereby what we preach to the world, what we advocate, is not exemplified in our own church structures and lifestyles — thereby undercutting the impact of our advocacy. Things like climate change will not wait for long-term education, but surely such education — about the biblical call to care for the environment, about the extent of the earth's degradation as a result of human activity — must accompany our efforts at immediate response.

7. The final tension, and the most important theologically, is a dialectic familiar to the churches: God's initiative and our human response. Much discussion about advocacy emphasizes what we accomplish, and human effort is obviously essential. Seen in faith perspective, however, such effort is understood as a response to what God has done, is doing, and will do — as participation in *God's* mission. Getting this theological point straight, in my experience, has very practical benefits: It is a check against self-righteousness. It is a spur to working with others. It is the foundation for deep hopefulness.

11. Chapman, *Faith, Power, and Politics*, p. 71.

And it is a reminder to ground all that we do in study of Scripture and in prayer. One of the things that has undermined the NCC's social witness in recent years is inadequate theological and biblical foundation, which is usually a sign that we are pushing an ideological agenda rather than opening ourselves to genuine wrestling with our heritage of faith.

Social advocates in the church are often (disparagingly) called "activists." At its best, however, Christian advocacy is not an anxious human effort to create a better world, but a testimony to our faith in God's power to overcome evil. "An activist," Henri Nouwen once wrote, "wants to heal, restore, redeem, and re-create, but those acting within the house of God point through their action to the healing, restoring, redeeming, and re-creating presence of God."[12]

I hope that this list of tensions, drawn from my own experience, can be important for others involved in advocacy through ecumenical organizations. I am committed to this kind of ministry, not because it is efficient, but because I am convinced that the willingness of Christians to act trustfully with differences is itself our most significant witness against the forces of fragmentation and exclusion. It is, itself, a political witness.

Examples of Convergence

In 2008 the NCC produced "A Social Creed for the 21st Century," marking the one hundredth anniversary of a famous, ecumenically affirmed Social Creed that contributed to the churches' policies on economic justice for two generations.[13] This new Social Creed, which I commend for serious study, should not be mistaken for an "ecumenical social doctrine." There is no such thing. It does, however, reflect areas of convergence that have become part of the substance of the churches' life together.

Another example of such convergence is a list of "Christian Principles for an Election Year," drafted by the NCC's Justice and Advocacy Commission in 2004 and subsequently endorsed for distribution by the council's Governing Board.[14] Typical of many ecumenical statements, these prin-

12. In Henri J. M. Nouwen, *Christ Our Hope: Daily Lenten Devotions* (St. Louis, Mo.: Creative Communications, 2007).

13. "A Social Creed for the 21st Century," at http://www.ncccusa.org/news/ga2007 .socialcreed.html.

14. "Christian Principles in an Election Year," at http://www.ncccusa.org/electionyear principlesguide.pdf.

ciples take the form of "middle axioms": principles that are more specific than biblical norms (e.g., love your neighbor and care for the poor), but not as specific as pieces of legislation, on which Christians can surely have differing opinions. I leave it to readers to decide whether these are an example of the ecumenical movement being too political or of the churches expressing together their understanding of how the gospel bears on contemporary society:

1. *War is contrary to the will of God.* While the use of violent force may, at times, be a necessity of last resort, Christ pronounces his blessing on peacemakers. We look for political leaders who will make peace with justice a top priority and who will actively seek non-violent solutions to conflict.

2. *God calls us to live in communities shaped by peace and cooperation.* We reject policies that abandon large segments of our inner-city and rural populations to hopelessness. We look for political leaders who will rebuild our communities and bring an end to the cycles of violence and killing.

3. *God created us for each other, and thus our security depends on the well-being of our global neighbors.* We look for political leaders for whom a foreign policy based on cooperation and global justice is an urgent concern.

4. *God calls us to be advocates for those who are most vulnerable in our society.* We look for political leaders who yearn for economic justice and who will seek to reduce the growing disparity between rich and poor.

5. *Each human being is created in the image of God and is of infinite worth.* We look for political leaders who actively promote racial justice and equal opportunity for everyone.

6. *The earth belongs to God and is intrinsically good.* We look for political leaders who recognize the earth's goodness, champion environmental justice, and uphold our responsibility to be stewards of God's creation.

7. *Christians have a biblical mandate to welcome strangers.* We look for political leaders who will pursue fair immigration policies and speak out against xenophobia.

8. *Those who follow Christ are called to heal the sick.* We look for political leaders who will support adequate, affordable, and accessible health care for all.

9. *Because of the transforming power of God's grace, all humans are called to be in right relationship with each other.* We look for political leaders

who seek a restorative, not retributive, approach to the criminal justice system and the individuals within it.

10. *Providing enriched learning environments for all of God's children is a moral imperative.* We look for political leaders who will advocate for equal educational opportunity and abundant funding for children's services.

CHAPTER 8

What Is the Way Forward for Catholic-Protestant Relations?

with Father Thomas Ryan[1]

There was a time in this country, not so long ago, when Roman Catholics were reluctant even to enter a Protestant church and when Protestants frowned at the very thought of a Catholic in the White House. So this chapter on Protestant-Catholic relations must surely begin with thanksgiving for what the Spirit has done to bring us closer to one another.

It is our experience, however, that much of the ecumenical momentum generated by the Second Vatican Council (1962-1965) has been lost, that local relations between Roman Catholics and ecumenically engaged Protestants, once the focus of real energy and passion, have reached a kind of plateau. There is cooperation between congregations and parishes in many places (and certainly less suspicion than a half-century ago), but few are doing all that is permitted, even encouraged, by official church declarations. Worse, we see signs of possible new estrangement brought on by differing perspectives on the culture-war issues of the day.

This chapter, the product of our friendship and collaboration since the early 1980s, is an attempt to suggest a way forward ecumenically by focusing on local communities. Behind it is our agreement with a principle first articulated during the formation of the World Council of Churches: "We may not pretend that the existing unity among Christians is greater than in fact it

1. Father Tom Ryan is a Catholic priest of the Community of St. Paul, known widely as the Paulists. He directs that community's North American Office for Ecumenical and Interfaith Relations, and is one of the most passionate, persistent, and practical voices anywhere for the unity of Christ's body.

is; but we should act upon it so far as it is already a reality."[2] The national and international dialogues between our churches, Catholic and Protestant, have not yet reached the point where we can share the eucharist, but they have cleared the way for a great deal of common life — and we should act on that.

We've Come a Long Way

It is important not to forget too easily just how much, and how quickly, things have changed! Michael, who was born in 1949, remembers growing up in small Iowa towns where religious activities that included the tiny Catholic parishes were, at best, rare. He cannot recall setting foot inside a Catholic church or meeting a local priest until his high school years. Catholicism was, for him as a youth, a kind of secret society, shrouded in taboos and rituals that seemed decidedly strange. He probably knew that Roman Catholics were Christians, but the Catholic Church *felt* like a different religion.

Tom also grew up in a small midwestern town, just across the border from Iowa in Minnesota, in the same years as Michael. His parents were daily communicants at mass, and the family lived a block from Saint Mary's, their parish church and school. From kindergarten on, Tom's whole social matrix was Roman Catholic. The Protestant kids in town went to the public school across the street from Saint Mary's, but about the only time the public and parochial school kids interacted was in sporting events — on opposing teams, as seemed fitting. It was only in his high school years that Tom began occasionally to mix socially with some of his Protestant peers; but then, when he went off to a Catholic college, it was back again to the Catholic fold.

It is also worth remembering that the nineteenth-century founders of the denomination in which Michael is a member, the Christian Church (Disciples of Christ), shared with other Protestants of the era an antipathy toward Catholics. The most prominent of the early Disciples, Alexander Campbell, spoke of the Roman Catholic Church as "the Great Apostasy foretold by prophets and apostles," and gave thanks for "the Lutheran effort to dethrone the Man of Sin"[3] — a position that certainly inhibits contact

2. Quoted in W. A. Visser 't Hooft, *The Genesis and Formation of the World Council of Churches* (Geneva: WCC, 1982), p. 55.

3. Alexander Campbell, *The Christian System* (St. Louis: Christian Publishing Co., 1835), p. 3.

with Catholic neighbors. On the other side of the coin, a papal encyclical from 1928 declared it "unlawful" for Catholics to engage in or support ecumenical endeavors, "for if they do so they will be giving countenance to a false Christianity, quite alien from the one Church of Christ. . . . the union of Christians can only be promoted by promoting the return to the one true Church of Christ of those who are separated from it."[4]

This kind of thinking began to change in America in the years after World War II, when the two of us were growing up; but the real breakthrough came with Vatican II and its seminal *Decree on Ecumenism* (1964). The *Decree's* famous first paragraph declares that division among the many churches "openly contradicts the will of Christ, scandalizes the world, and damages that most holy cause, the preaching of the gospel to every creature."[5] The bishops go on to affirm that all who have been incorporated into Christ through baptism in another Christian community "are brought into real, though imperfect, communion with the Catholic Church."[6] They participate in Christ's saving work, not in spite of their community of faith, but through it. This is official confirmation of what our experience also teaches: that the two of us are brothers in Jesus Christ.

This may be familiar ground for many readers; but the *Decree's* implications for local church life seem not to be so well known. The *Decree* exhorts Catholics, lay as well as clergy, "to take an active and intelligent part in the work of ecumenism" by

- avoiding judgments or actions that caricature other Christians or otherwise make mutual relations more difficult;
- getting to know the history and internal life of other churches;
- cooperating in mission on behalf of "the common good of humanity";
- undertaking renewal of their own church, where needed; and
- engaging in common prayer.[7]

The last point, in particular, is reinforced by the great encyclical letter of Pope John Paul II, *Ut Unum Sint* ("That All May Be One," 1995), which reiterates that the Catholic Church is "irrevocably" committed to the ecumenical

4. *Mortalium Animos,* at http://www.papalencyclicals.net/Pius11/P11MORTA.HTM.

5. *Unitatis Redintegratio* (Decree on Ecumenism), par. 1, at http://www.vatican.va/archive/hist_councils/ii_vatican_council/documents/vat-ii_decree_19641121_unitatis-redintegratio_en.html.

6. Decree on Ecumenism, par. 3.

7. Decree on Ecumenism, par. 4.

venture and identifies prayer as "the soul of the whole ecumenical movement. . . . If Christians, despite their divisions, can grow ever more united in
common prayer around Christ, they will grow in the awareness of how little
divides them in comparison with what unites them." The encyclical specifically encourages participation in the Week of Prayer for Christian Unity
(though it observes that there are also many other occasions when Christians
are led to pray together), and says that relations among the various churches
"call for every possible form of practical cooperation at all levels: pastoral,
cultural and social, as well as that of witnessing to the gospel message." All
of this, according to the Pope, enables still-separated Christians to know
each other better, and thus hastens the day when this "real, but imperfect,
communion" will be expressed in fuller unity. "A century ago," he writes,
"who could even have imagined such a thing?"[8]

The astonishing convergence set forth in these texts is given more comprehensive and detailed treatment in the *Directory for the Application of
Principles and Norms of Ecumenism,* released with the authority of the Pope
in 1993.[9] It indicates that the following activities are not only allowed but
encouraged for local parishes:

- sharing in prayer and liturgical worship (pars. 102-120);
- reading lessons or preaching, when invited, as part of the liturgical celebration of another church (par. 118);
- inviting, upon permission of the bishop, the minister of another church
to read a lesson or offer a prayer as part of the celebration of baptism
(par. 97);
- joining with other Christians in services that reaffirm our baptismal
vows (par. 96);
- cooperating in the study and propagation of the Bible and in other forms
of Christian education (par. 161);
- setting up committees "in more or less permanent form" to promote and
facilitate ecumenical relations (par. 163);
- joining with others in local councils of churches (pars. 166-171); and
- cooperating "in pastoral care, in evangelization, and in . . . service of

8. *Ut Unum Sint,* pars. 3, 21, 22, 24, 40, and 45, at http://www.vatican.va/holy_father/john
_paul_ii/encyclicals/documents/hf_jp-ii_enc_25051995_ut-unum-sint_en.html.

9. *Directory for the Application of Principles and Names of Ecumenism,* at http://www
.vatican.va/roman_curia/pontifical_councils/chrstuni/general-docs/rc_pc_chrstuni_doc
_19930325_directory_en.html.

charity to a world that is struggling to realize its ideals of justice, peace, and love" (par. 161).

"Christians," in the words of the *Directory*, "cannot close their hearts to the crying needs of our contemporary world. The contribution they are able to make to all the areas of human life . . . will be more effective when they make it together, and when they are seen to be united in making it. Hence, they will want to do everything together that is allowed by their faith."[10] We hear in this an echo of what is known in the ecumenical movement as the Lund Principle: Churches should "act together in all matters except those in which deep differences of conviction compel them to act separately."[11]

Some things, of course, are *not* permitted at this stage of our pilgrimage toward one another — including, most painfully, the sharing of the eucharist. But, as Diane Kessler writes in her "Protestant reading" of the *Directory,* churches of the Reformation can focus on such prohibitions "or we can concentrate on the positives — on what we can do now together, on the encouragements — and get going. . . . In fact, if every diocese around the world took fully to heart all that is now possible ecumenically, other churches would be scrambling to catch up with the Roman Catholic Church, and we would be ahead of where we are now."[12]

We agree! "We may not pretend that the existing unity among Christians is greater than in fact it is; but we should act upon it so far as it is already a reality."

Recommendations for Local Collaboration

Over the years, the two of us, with these official teachings in mind, have made our own recommendations for local collaboration between Catholics and Protestants. Michael offered the following list while participating in the international dialogue between the Roman Catholic Church and the Disciples of Christ:

- pray for neighboring congregations/parishes by name on a regular basis;
- make it a priority to join for prayer and worship on special occasions;

10. *Directory,* par. 162.

11. Oliver S. Tomkins, ed., *The Third World Conference on Faith and Order* (London: SCM, 1953), p. 16.

12. Diane C. Kessler, "The New Catholic Ecumenical Directory: A Protestant Reading," *Ecumenical Review* 47 (October 1995): 420.

- invite one another to social events in the congregation/parish;
- organize joint educational programs for children, youth, and adults;
- teach about the other community in our own education classes;
- share facilities and resources when the other has need;
- look for opportunities to make common public witness to Jesus Christ; and
- participate in one another's baptisms, with permission, as a sign that a person is baptized into the one body of Christ.

Tom has gone even further in recommending that parishes enter into "ecumenical covenants" with neighboring Protestant congregations in order "to express together a shared Christian life to the extent current circumstances permit." In addition to the points on Michael's list, Tom has encouraged Catholic parishes, as part of such covenants, to

- offer public intercessions for the concerns of the partner congregation(s), especially for persons being baptized or confirmed;
- form a support group for interchurch couples;
- invite a designated member of the partner congregation to attend meetings of the parish council or other governing committee;
- display bulletins, newsletters, and similar materials of the covenant partner;
- initiate service projects with the partner congregation in response to local needs, such as transportation for the elderly and disabled and care for refugee families;
- take care that new clergy coming to the parish support the principles of the covenant and affirm the search for Christian unity as priority; and
- renew the covenant annually (in concert with the partner congregation), amending it as both see appropriate.[13]

To take one example, in the Highlands area of Louisville, Kentucky, twenty-five congregations, including six Roman Catholic parishes, are part of Highlands Community Ministries, which formed in 1970 (during the heady years following the Second Vatican Council). The participating congregations have entered into a covenant — "promises that we make to one another before God" — to pray for one another and to join in regular oc-

---

13. Thomas Ryan, *A Survival Guide for Ecumenically Minded Christians* (Ottawa: Novalis, 1989), pp. 161-63.

casions of common worship; to share facilities and resources, both human and material; to serve together the needs of persons in the community; and "to witness together to our faith in Jesus Christ, who came not to be served but to serve." The covenant includes a shared affirmation of faith, a common baptismal certificate, and a preamble in which the participating churches "proclaim the measure of unity which has been achieved in our life together."[14]

We believe that these recommendations, and the Louisville example, are fully consistent with the approach to Christian unity articulated by Cardinal Joseph Ratzinger, later to become Pope Benedict XVI, in his 1988 book *Church, Ecumenism, and Politics*. Building on the work of Protestant scholar Oscar Cullmann, Ratzinger urges the diverse churches in ecumenical dialogue

> to take the poison out of it and to receive precisely the positive element from this diversity — naturally in the hope that finally the division will cease to be a division at all and is merely a polarity without opposition. . . . [Such dialogue involves] learning afresh from the other as other while respecting his or her otherness. As people who are divided, we can also be one.[15]

A first step, he continues, is to discover and publicly acknowledge "the various kinds of unity that already exist and that in truth are not inconsiderable." After that, it is "a question of putting this existing unity to work, of making it actual and broadening it. This would naturally include a diversity of forms of encounter at all levels (ministers, theologians, laypeople) and of joint action."[16]

One of the historical forms of ministry that members of Tom's community, the Paulist Fathers, have exercised over the years is the preaching of what are called "parish missions." This begins with the missioner preaching at all the weekend masses and continues for the next three or four days with a daytime event for seniors and an evening Service of the Word, with homily, for the working folks.

Early in his ministry, Tom began to ask himself how an "ecumenical

14. See the Highlands Community Ministers website at http://hcmlouisville.org/about-us.
15. Cardinal Joseph Ratzinger, *Church, Ecumenism, and Politics* (New York: Crossroad, 1988), pp. 139-40.
16. Ratzinger, *Church, Ecumenism, and Politics*, p. 140.

spin" might be given to these parish missions. His prayer and reflection led him to conceive of undertaking these missions with a Protestant preaching partner, going not only to a Catholic parish but to co-sponsoring congregations of different denominations on successive evenings. Tom invited a good friend, the assistant pastor of the Anglican cathedral in Montreal (where he was living), to be his co-missioner, and together they began to promote the idea to councils of churches in Canadian cities and provinces, reserving a few weeks in their calendars each year to devote to these ecumenical missions.

One of their first mission invitations came from four congregations of different denominations in a suburb of Edmonton, Alberta. On a given Sunday, they individually preached in one or two services in each church, inviting the members to gather in each other's churches over the next four evenings for prayer and fellowship — to get into each other's "rooms" in the Christian household in order to develop a "family feeling." During the course of each following day, they offered an event: a prayer breakfast for those on their way to work, with a talk on the theme of "Taking God to Work," or a Bible study or faith-sharing experience for stay-at-home parents and seniors.

At each evening Service of the Word, after a sermon preached jointly by Tom and his friend, all those gathered were invited to come forward and engage together in a ritual action expressing their shared faith. On the first evening, they dipped a hand in the water of the baptismal font, turned to the person behind them, and applied the water to his or her forehead with these words from Ephesians: "Maintain the unity of the Spirit in the bond of peace" (Eph. 4:3). On the second night, the people approached and reverenced (offered some words or gestures showing respect for) an open Bible. On the third night, they reverenced a large cross. And on the closing night, in the spirit of the theme of being sent forth in mission, they lit tapers from the Easter candle as a sign of their readiness to carry the light of Christ back into the little world under their feet and within their reach — together.

During the course of the mission, those involved in ministries in the co-sponsoring congregations met in affinity groups — youth ministers, liturgists, administrators, social justice leaders, Christian education coordinators, and the like — in order to share with one another the nature of their ministry, some resources they have found particularly helpful, and whether there are parts of their ministry that they might be able to do better together rather than alone. After spending time in groups, they returned to the plenary gathering to focus on that final question: What can we do better together than as single congregations?

Members from the different congregations testified that the mission had been an occasion for them to create relationships, to come to a clearer realization that the faith they share is much broader and deeper than anything that still divides them, and to affirm that there are things they can and should be doing together. They also decided that they wanted to keep it going. In 2014 these congregations will celebrate twenty-five years of co-sponsoring an annual ecumenical mission. In the years since that initial mission, each of the congregations in rotation has invited a preacher from their own Christian tradition, with everyone invited to their church for that year's mission. Pastors and members of these churches bear witness that their deepening relationships have impacted the way they engage in mission in their part of Edmonton.

Tom has since moved back to the United States and carries on these renewal events under the title "Gospel Call."[17] He has found these the most energizing and fulfilling of his numerous ecumenical and interfaith activities because they reach people at the grassroots — and not just individuals but whole congregations. They deepen Christians' sense of identity and solidarity with one another where they live, and enable the co-sponsoring congregations to envision their ministry differently, identifying concrete ways in which their congregations can act together in the future.

Theological dialogues are of real importance, and we — Michael and Tom — give thanks for those who engage in them. But the crux of ecumenical work is to deepen the experience of the unity we have in Christ through personal relationships, *locally* as well as globally. In our experience, any advance in the search for the visible unity of the church has come about because relationships of trust and confidence have developed between people from the various traditions involved. Ecumenism is so often thought of in terms of programs and meetings, which can seem burdensome in the midst of busy schedules. Thus, it is vital to keep in mind that, at root, it is all about relationships. Are we willing to make time for the Spirit to work in us by spending time with others? It could be as simple as picking up the phone and inviting a local pastor to dinner.

To put it another way, "ecumenical" is short-hand for a way of being Christian that seeks to know how God is working in the lives of those who have come to love and follow Christ in churches other than our own. Perhaps we can call it an ecumenical Golden Rule: Try to understand others, even as you would be understood by them. Instead of mentally defining "those Catholics" or "those evangelicals" or "those mainliners" on the basis of what

17. Information at http://www.tomryancsp.org/gospelcall.htm.

we have heard in our own communities, ecumenical Christians seek to know others in the particularity of their praying, their serving, and their believing. In the words of the Highlands Community Ministries covenant, "Trust and understanding have grown through our work together. We have become committed to one another. We have come to recognize that there is, indeed, 'one Lord, one faith, one baptism, one God and Father of all, who is above all and through all and in all' (Eph. 4:5-6)."[18]

Ongoing Scandal

We noted at the beginning of this chapter that there has been marked improvement in Protestant-Catholic relations when compared with the situation a half century ago, and the examples we have cited bear this out. At the same time, we agree with Cardinal Walter Kasper, former head of the Vatican office for promoting Christian unity, that "there is now much disenchantment at unfulfilled expectations."[19] In other words, while the members of our churches have reason to be thankful for advances in unity, we also have reason to ask why more has not been done. Why have the directives of Vatican II not been more energetically implemented? Why have Protestants not welcomed Catholic neighbors more warmly? Why have the leaders of these Reformation churches not encouraged such welcome more vigorously? Why have the results of Catholic-Protestant dialogues not been more widely distributed and joyfully taught in our churches? Why are there not more covenants between Catholic parishes and Protestant congregations? Why are we not doing all that is now permitted?

Cardinal Kasper's successor at the Pontifical Council for Promoting Christian Unity, Cardinal Kurt Koch, gives powerful voice to our conviction: "That Christians who believe in Jesus Christ as the Redeemer of the world and are baptized into his one body continue to live in churches separated from one another is the great offense which Christendom still offers to the world today and which deserves to be called a scandal."[20] We pray that the Holy Spirit will convict Protestants and Catholics from Seattle to Miami, from Boston to San Diego, of this offense and lead us in each local setting

18. At the Highland Community Ministries website.

19. Cardinal Walter Kasper, "May They All Be One? But How? A Vision of Christian Unity for the Next Generation," *Ecumenical Trends* 40 (April 2011): 4.

20. Cardinal Kurt Koch, "Fundamental Aspects of Ecumenism and Future Perspectives," an unpublished paper presented November 3, 2011, at the Catholic University of America.

to "act together in all matters except those in which deep differences of conviction compel [us] to act separately" — until the day when we are truly united in the name of our common Lord and Savior. Fifty years ago, who could even have imagined such a thing?!

CHAPTER 9

How Can the Orthodox Help Others Understand Them Better?

An Open Letter

Dear Brothers and Sisters in the Orthodox churches:

Grace to you and peace in the name of the one triune God, Father, Son, and Holy Spirit.

Please accept this as an open letter from a Protestant Christian who highly values the participation — the leadership — of Orthodox Christians in the ecumenical movement. I offer a *letter* rather than an essay because I think we need more speaking *with* one another and less speaking *about* one another. How many times, at ecumenical conferences, have I been part of hallway conversations among Protestants lamenting the positions of those "obstreperous Orthodox." And I imagine that Orthodox participants at ecumenical meetings have had similar conversations about "recalcitrant Protestants." Surely we honor one another and our common Lord by our willingness to "speak the truth in love" in order that together we might "grow up in every way into him who is the head, into Christ" (Eph. 4:15).

I make this an *open* letter because there is much in it that I hope Protestants will take to heart. To them I say, "The Orthodox are not just exotica that you want 'to include' for the sake of diversity but then try to work around!" Protestant churches, if I may put it this way, are the evangelical tip of an orthodox iceberg. I firmly believe that God has blessed these churches, churches in which I have come to know Christ and seek to do ministry in his name, with gifts needed for the building up of the body; but apart from you, apart from the tradition you have endeavored to preserve and embody, our distinctive witness has no foundation.

In this open letter I will name five misperceptions of the Orthodox

Church that, in my experience, are held by many of your Christian neighbors here in the United States. I say *mis*perceptions because I am convinced that these ideas are generally based on false understandings, even plain old ignorance. But, in my judgment, Orthodox often contribute to these misunderstandings in ways I will try to identify.

I do not have in mind specific issues of dispute, such as the ordination of women. Rather, I want to address those things that keep us from speaking constructively with one another about such issues. May God use these words that we may "welcome one another, just as Christ has welcomed [us], to the glory of God" (Rom. 15:7).

Misperception 1: The Orthodox Church is "foreign," not truly American.
Part of the problem, of course, is ignorance of history. I have been privileged to worship in the Cathedral of St. Michael the Archangel in Sitka, Alaska, a church first built in 1848. As you know, the history of Orthodox missionary work in Alaska goes back well before that. Orthodox from Russia were preaching the gospel of Jesus Christ on what is now U.S. soil four decades before my own Protestant denomination, the Christian Church (Disciples of Christ), was born on the American frontier! And this is not a singular example. Immigrant-based Orthodox parishes were established from New York to New Orleans to San Francisco by the mid-nineteenth century. No Protestant seminary should teach *American* church history without doing justice to this Orthodox presence, even as I trust that you teach about Protestants in your own theological education.

The real issue, however, goes deeper than history — to the question of identity. I vividly recall a National Council of Churches visit to the Malankara Orthodox Church when our delegation asked, "Are you an Indian church with a presence in America or an American church with deep roots in India?" and then watched the room divide as our hosts tried to answer. I imagine most Orthodox, especially those in churches that have been here longer, would agree in principle with Father Tom FitzGerald that "Orthodoxy in the United States may no longer be viewed simply as a diaspora composed primarily of immigrants . . . [but] as an emerging local church comprised primarily of American citizens of a wide variety of racial, ethnic, and religious backgrounds."[1] But, as you know better than I, this remains a real struggle.

---

1. Thomas FitzGerald, "Orthodoxy in the United States," in Fotios K. Litsas, ed., *A Companion to the Greek Orthodox Church* (New York: Greek Orthodox Archdiocese of North and South America, 1984), p. 177.

It is not my place or intent to comment extensively on internal Orthodox concerns. I do, however, want to name the issue for those Protestants who may be reading this open letter.

At the beginning of the twentieth century, there was one North American diocese, containing the diversity of Orthodox communities; but by the 1920s (for complex historical reasons), multiple parallel jurisdictions emerged, each now directed toward preserving a national/cultural heritage. This, as Orthodox scholars repeatedly observe, is a grave violation of Orthodox ecclesiology. It belies the essential unity of the church in each place and contributes to the (mis)perception that Orthodoxy is not truly American. As the Orthodox bishops in this country put it in 1994, the idea of being diaspora churches "diminishes the fullness of the faith that we have lived and experienced for the past two hundred years."[2] The church is apostolic not because it remains tied to places where the apostles preached and established churches, but because it continues the apostolic vocation in new settings. Deep cultural roots in Greece, Russia, Serbia, Romania, Syria, Egypt, Armenia, India, or Ethiopia? Of course. But if your center of gravity is elsewhere, others will continue to suspect that Orthodoxy is a "foreign" version of Christianity, not fully rooted in U.S. soil.

With that in mind, let me say how thankful I, a non-Orthodox, am for the new Assembly of Canonical Bishops in North and South America. This regular gathering will surely result in greater cooperation among Orthodox jurisdictions, and, with the help of God, may lead to even more visible oneness. An Orthodox Church that is inclusive of the many national and cultural communities that inhabit this continent would be "American" in the deepest sense. And it would be a powerful witness to Protestants, implicitly indicting us for our own unbiblical fragmentation.

I can't help but add that it also helps to be fully engaged partners in the National Council of Churches (NCC). Through participation in the council, churches demonstrate their concern for the mission needs of *this* nation and learn from one another how to live in this culture without succumbing to it.

Misperception 2: The Orthodox Church is not really committed to the ecumenical movement.
Once again, a little history can help. The first great document of modern ecumenism was, arguably, an encyclical sent in 1920 by the Holy Synod of

2. Quoted in Leonid Kishkovsky, "Orthodoxy in America: Diaspora or Church," at http:// oca.org/holy-synod/statements/fr-kishkovsky/orthodoxy-in-america-diaspora-or-church.

the Church of Constantinople "unto the churches of Christ everywhere." Its irenic language is worth recalling: "Our own church holds that rapprochement between the various Christian churches and fellowship between them is not excluded by the doctrinal differences which exist between them. In our opinion, such a rapprochement is highly desirable and necessary."[3] The encyclical goes on to call for such things as student exchanges between seminaries of different churches, mutual assistance in the cause of charity, a uniform calendar for the celebration of the great Christian feasts, and a "league (fellowship) between the churches" *(koinonia ton ekklesion)* — an idea which led eventually to the founding of the World Council of Churches (WCC).

No list of the outstanding ecumenical leaders of the twentieth century would be complete without Patriarch Athenagoras and Archbishop Iakovos (hierarchs with strong American connections), along with Archbishop Germanos of Thyateria, Father Georges Florovsky, Professor Nikos Nissiotis, Metropolitan Paulos Mar Gregorios, and Archbishop Anastasios of Albania — to name only a few. When I became general secretary of the National Council of Churches in 2008, three of the council's five program commissions had a member of the Greek Orthodox Church as chairperson or vice chairperson, and the president of the NCC was the Armenian Orthodox Archbishop Vicken Aykazian. I point this out to Protestants at every opportunity.

Protestant suspicions of Orthodox ecumenical commitment are, however, at least somewhat understandable. During my time at the NCC, the financial contribution the council received from the United Methodist Church, by itself, was roughly *fifty* times that of all nine Orthodox churches combined. Guess which church felt that it was more committed to the work of the National Council?

But, once again, the issue runs deeper. Protestants think of the one church of Jesus Christ as fragmented into various denominations, and so they seek unity (the stated goal of the ecumenical movement) through dialogue aimed at shared mission and mutual recognition. As you are well aware, no Orthodox church thinks of itself as a denomination! For you, the unity Christians have in Christ is manifested in the historical and apostolic church. There is but one church in history — which means that the ecumenical problem, as you see it, is not fragmentation but schism, a falling

3. "Unto the Churches of Christ Everywhere," in Michael Kinnamon and Brian E. Cope, eds., *The Ecumenical Movement: An Anthology of Key Texts and Voices* (Grand Rapids: Eerdmans, 1997), p. 12.

away from the truth of the apostolic faith. To use Father Florovsky's famous distinction, Protestants emphasize "ecumenism in space," the integration of existing churches, while Orthodox emphasize "ecumenism in time," the common confession of the faith of the church through the ages[4] — a faith which you believe you have preserved. If I am not mistaken, these differing conceptions of ecumenism often leave you feeling like a square peg in a round hole, like outsiders in organizations still dominated by Protestants, many of whom are unaware of these divergent conceptions.

The underlying issues will not, cannot, be dealt with quickly. Ecumenism is an often-frustrating journey in faith that follows God's timetable, not our own. It would give credibility to our faith and our efforts, however, if others could see more signs of progress along the way.

Isn't it possible, for example, for Christians to answer the call of the 1920 encyclical by adopting a common date for Easter? A major step in this direction was taken in 1997 when a WCC-sponsored conference in Aleppo, Syria, offered three simple, yet profound, recommendations:

- adhere to the decision of the Council of Nicea [325] to celebrate Easter on the first Sunday following the first full moon after the spring equinox, thus maintaining the biblical association between the Passion and Passover;
- agree to use the most current scientific methods to analyze the astronomical date (which is consistent with Nicea); and
- use the meridian of Jerusalem, due to its centrality in the Passion narrative, as the point of reference for these calculations.[5]

Easter, Christians confess, is the ultimate expression of God's reconciling, unifying love. And yet, almost every year, the Christian community is divided over when to celebrate this divine event, thus undermining our proclamation of its meaning for the life of the world!

Over and over I have seen students, excited by their first encounter with the ecumenical vision of unity in Christ, grow disillusioned when "nothing seems to change." Needless to say, the Orthodox are not the only ones responsible for ecumenical stagnation. But you do at times get blamed

4. See, e.g., Georges Florovsky, "Obedience and Witness," in Robert C. Mackie and Charles C. West., eds., *The Sufficiency of God* (Philadelphia: Westminster, 1963), pp. 66-67.

5. "Towards a Common Date of Easter," par. 11, at http://www.oikoumene.org/en/resources/documents/wcc-commissions/faith-and-order-commission/i-unity-the-church-and-its-mission/towards-a-common-date-for-easter/towards-a-common-date-for-easter.html.

for it. So how energizing it would be if you would take the lead on an initiative, first proposed by the Ecumenical Patriarchate, that could affect every Christian.

Misperception 3: The Orthodox Church is not involved in struggles for justice and peace in the world.
People who make such a claim, and I hear it a lot, apparently don't know about the vigorous defense of God's creation, the concern for ecological justice, displayed by Patriarch Bartholomew, who, as you know, is the primary spiritual leader of the Orthodox Christian world. The "Green Patriarch" has written and spoken extensively about "environmental sin," which "demands a radical transformation of the way we perceive the natural world and a tangible change in the way we choose to live."[6] And in seminars and colloquia that he has organized around the world, His All-Holiness has insisted on the link between "caring for the poor and caring for the earth."[7] None of this is news to you, but remember that I want Protestants to read this letter too.

The Patriarch, as I understand it, is giving voice to a powerful moral tradition in Orthodoxy, one rooted in biblical and patristic sources — including St. John Chrysostom, who famously spoke of the relationship between the "sacrament of the altar" and the "sacrament of the brother." For me, one of the best expressions of this tradition is Father Alexander Schmemann's wonderful little book *For the Life of the World*. It is the *world*, he emphasizes, that is the object of God's saving love. Christians are called "to live eucharistically," giving thanks to God for the gift of creation through active care for nature and neighbor. Those who recognize the world as shot through with the presence of God will never restrict the interests and concerns of the church to a compartment labeled "religious."[8]

As a seminary professor, I have insisted to my students that ethics and theology must not be separated, that our social witness must be grounded in our faith and worship; and I have often quoted such Orthodox scholars as Stanley Harakas and Emmanuel Clapsis when doing so. The church is not a pious huddle. But neither is it a social action coalition. The Orthodox, at your best, help the whole church hold this balance.

6. Patriarch Bartholomew, "The Orthodox Church and the Environmental Crisis," in Lyndsay Moseley, ed., *Holy Ground: A Gathering of Voices on Caring for Creation* (San Francisco: Sierra Club Books, 2008), p. 38.

7. Patriarch Bartholomew, "The Orthodox Church," p. 40.

8. Alexander Schmemann, *For the Life of the World* (Crestwood, N.Y.: St. Vladimir's Seminary Press, 1963), pp. 11-22.

Of course, the church is not always at its best. All of our communities have a tendency to turn inward, focusing on the internal life of the church rather than on the church's participation in God's mission for the world. I suspect that Archbishop Anastasios had this in mind in his sermon at the 2006 assembly of the WCC. "Woe to us," declared His Eminence, "if, in the twenty-first century, we again relinquish the initiative for social justice to others, as we have done in past centuries, while we confine ourselves to opulent rituals, and to our usual alliance with the powerful."[9] I don't think he was speaking only to Protestants.

Once again, participation in conciliar life, locally as well as nationally, can help. At their best, councils of churches are settings where churches can multiply their witness and expand their agenda by responding to issues of social and environmental justice together. A key principle of conciliar life is that each member should take seriously what other members regard as important. We may not agree with the positions of other churches, but we do agree to take seriously the things that matter to them. My own American-born denomination, if left on its own, would likely pay little corporate attention to the plight of Christians in Egypt or Turkey. But because this matters to you, our conciliar partners, it demands our active concern.

Orthodox, at times, have had a tendency to focus rather exclusively on issues of particular importance to your communities, thus contributing to the (mis)perception that you are not fully involved in the struggles for justice and peace. I urge you to see the racism experienced by African Americans or the poverty of rural America (not exactly the heartland of Orthodoxy) or immigration policies aimed at Latin Americans as if these things were happening to you. Because in the fellowship of a council, they are.

Misperception 4: The Orthodox Church is stuck in the past.
This is where you are really swimming upstream in U.S. culture. A culture that revels in the present and treats yesterday as obsolete will have little appreciation for the Orthodox emphasis on tradition. My own denomination, the Disciples of Christ, began as part of the nineteenth-century Restoration Movement in American Protestantism, a movement that sought to "restore" the New Testament church by jumping over the "distortions" that arose during nearly two thousand years of church history. So you can imag-

---

9. Anastasios of Albania, "Opening Sermon," in Luis N. Rivera-Pagan, ed., *God, In Your Grace: Official Report of the Ninth Assembly of the World Council of Churches* (Geneva: WCC, 2007), p. 59.

ine how my Disciples ancestors regarded a church that looks for authority to councils of the fourth, fifth, sixth, seventh, and eighth centuries.

As a seminary professor, I was forever saying to students from my church, "You *receive* the faith, passed down to you as a sacred inheritance. You don't get to invent it in each new generation!" And I have greatly valued the presence of Orthodox in ecumenical settings because you insist on making that point. Liberal Protestants, including a good many of my students, pride themselves these days on being counter-cultural, when, of course, it is your emphasis on tradition that is truly counter-cultural in this setting.

Still, I think there is a challenge here for both Protestants *and* Orthodox. Metropolitan John Zizioulas, one of the leading contemporary Orthodox theologians, states it this way: "The Orthodox, on the one hand, do not seem to be willing to let their tradition (dogmatic or otherwise) be challenged enough by the problems of the day . . . , while the non-Orthodox, on the other hand, seem to be totally unwilling to take into consideration what has traditionally been conveyed to us. . . ."[10]

In this regard, it would help overcome Protestant (mis)perceptions if the *dynamic* character of tradition were underscored even more forcefully. One example of doing so came from the Orthodox delegates at the WCC's New Delhi Assembly (1961), who stressed that tradition is not "static restoration of old forms" but, rather, "a dynamic recovery of perennial ethos."[11] Or, as one of the bishops remarked at the Council of Carthage (257), "The Lord said, 'I am truth.' He did not say, 'I am custom.'" *Traditionalism*, in the well-known formulation of Jaroslav Pelikan, is "the dead faith of the living" — and it deserves to be rejected. But *tradition* is "the living faith of the dead" — and it is not stuck in the past.

Misperception 5: The Orthodox Church is spiritually arrogant.
This is the most difficult misperception, the one most likely to enflame passions all around; but, for that very reason, it must be discussed. I have been a professor in Protestant seminaries for more than a quarter century. Every time I have taught a course on ecumenism, students have gotten very upset — or disdainful — when they read how Orthodox claim to be *the* church,

10. John D. Zizioulas, "The Self-Understanding of the Orthodox and Their Participation in the Ecumenical Movement," in Gregory Edwards, ed., *The One and the Many* (Alhambra, Calif.: Sebastian Press, 2010), p. 325.
11. In Kinnamon and Cope, eds., *The Ecumenical Movement*, pp. 92-93.

refusing to recognize the ecclesial status of the communities of faith to which the students belong.

Please put yourselves in their place. The students know from long experience that their own Presbyterian or Methodist or Episcopal or Lutheran or Baptist or Disciples church confesses the living Christ; that their church's mission — guided, they believe, by the Holy Spirit — has borne spiritual fruit; that their congregations are filled with God-loving people who lead lives of faith and faithfulness; and that such persons as Martin Luther King Jr. and Reinhold Niebuhr have been nurtured by *their* communities. So it feels to them like pure arrogance for another church to say, "We don't recognize you as a church in the full theological sense of that term because your ministry isn't ordered as ours is, because you have not sufficiently adhered to traditions from the past."

Now let me acknowledge what my students often couldn't see — namely, the arrogance of *their* churches. To take a particularly painful example, planeloads of Protestants took off for Moscow and other Eastern European cities after 1989, eager "to convert the communists," completely overlooking or dismissing the local Orthodox churches. That, too, is arrogance in the guise of evangelism.

Given this tendency, it seems especially important for all Christian communions to repent of the ways in which they have given inadequate witness to "the faith once delivered to the saints." I think, for example, of an essay by Metropolitan Zizioulas in which he names the "disappointments and failures" that he sees in the history of Orthodoxy, including an inability, when dealing with other Christians, to "rise above the psychology of polemic in a true spirit of forgiveness and love"; a tendency to turn the Bible and the dogmas of the church into "formulae to be preserved rather than lived and experienced"; a marginalization of theology from ordinary life; an "infiltration of the Church by nationalism and sometimes ethnophyletism" (ecclesial tribalism based on ethnicity); and a general failure to love human beings as much as our Lord did.[12] I leave it to you to determine if these disappointments are on target. My point is simply that a willingness to offer such humble, self-critical confession goes a long way toward overcoming perceptions of arrogance.

This needs to be said carefully. I am certainly not suggesting that Orthodox should deny your own self-understanding by backing away from

12. John D. Zizioulas, "The Orthodox Church and the Third Millennium," in *The One and the Many*, pp. 390-91.

the claim to be the church, the historical form of Christ's abiding and acting presence. There are ways of making this claim, however, that, in my judgment, could contribute to ecumenical relationships rather than jeopardize them. Let me give a couple of brief examples.

The first is found in the Greek Orthodox response to the 1997 report of the NCC's Ecclesiology Study Task Force. The response reiterates that the Orthodox do not recognize some "ecclesial bodies" as churches, but then goes on to list ways in which Orthodox churches have been positively influenced by their involvement in the ecumenical movement. It has been good, in the words of the response, "to look at ourselves in new contexts and articulate our tradition in terms that heretofore had never been expected of us." Further, "participation in the ecumenical movement has been good because it has reminded us of the social dimension of our faith."[13]

Contrary to what some Protestants may think, this acknowledgement of learning from others is by no means unique. I think, for instance, of how the Ecumenical Patriarch Dimitrios, on the occasion of the WCC's twenty-fifth anniversary in 1973, publicly affirmed that the Orthodox have been "deeply enriched by the encounter with Western church life and theology, as well as by material assistance."[14] This willingness to receive gifts, as well as to offer your own, helps dispel misperceptions.

My other example is a grace-filled quotation from Metropolitan Zizioulas. "The Orthodox," he writes, "will never depart from their conviction that the Orthodox Church is the *Una Sancta*. . . . But ecumenical experience is taking away all triumphalism from such a conviction. The *Una Sancta* transmitted in and through tradition is not a possession of the Orthodox. It is a reality judging us all (eschatologically) and is something to be constantly received. The ecumenical movement," he concludes, "offers the context for such a re-reception that takes place in common with other Christians."[15] Presented in this way, Orthodox claims to be the church can be heard, even appreciated, by your Christian neighbors.

It remains only for me to pray, in the spirit of the apostle Paul, that God may grant us a greater measure of unity in truth in the years ahead. In all things, thanks be to God!

13. Unpublished paper.
14. "Declaration of the Ecumenical Patriarch on the Occasion of the 25th Anniversary of the World Council of Churches," *Ecumenical Review* 25 (October 1973): 477.
15. Zizioulas, "The Self-Understanding of the Orthodox," p. 330.

CHAPTER 10

How Are Interfaith Relationships as Challenging as They Are Necessary?

I am going to take it for granted that all of us are aware of the importance, the necessity, of positive interfaith relations. Christians in the United States now live — in our neighborhoods and, perhaps, in our families — with far greater religious diversity than that experienced by previous generations; and advances in transportation and communication put us in touch with people of other faiths around the world. In my own case, I have had a sister-in-law who is from a Buddhist family, another sister-in-law who is Jewish, and a daughter, Anna-Kapila, adopted as an infant, who was born in a Hindu ashram in the city of Mumbai.

More negatively, it should now be clear that such problems as climate change and poverty demand wide human collaboration. And, in case we missed these signs of the times, growth of sometimes-violent religious extremism underscores the urgent need for dialogue aimed at deeper understanding and cooperation on behalf of peace. The recent document "Christian Witness in a Multi-Religious World" — produced (somewhat astonishingly) by the World Council of Churches (WCC), the Vatican's Pontifical Council for Interreligious Dialogue, and the World Evangelical Alliance (WEA) — is very straightforward: "Christians should continue to build relationships of respect and trust with people of different religions so as to facilitate deeper mutual understanding, reconciliation, and cooperation for the common good."[1] The importance and appropriateness of such work should not be at issue.

1. "Christian Witness in a Multi-Religious World," Principle 12, at http://www.oikoumene .org/fileadmin/files/wcc-main/2011pdfs/ChristianWitness_recommendations.pdf.

This is not to say, however, that interfaith relationships are always easy or that engaging in them isn't challenging for U.S. Christians. In this chapter, I want to name five of those challenges in the hope that this might enable us to address them more effectively. I am not going to focus on challenges to specific dialogues, such as the difficulties for Jewish-Christian relations in this country that stem from differing perceptions of the conflict between Israelis and Palestinians.[2] Such matters are of great concern, but here my focus is on five more fundamental challenges that I have labeled "theological," "ecumenical," "moral," "missional," and "identity." A willingness to face such challenges may be an indication that Christians are moving beyond the excitement of initial interfaith encounter into a period of greater maturity in our relationships with other religious communities.

1. The Theological Challenge

The central challenge theologically is summed up in this question: What is the place of other religions in God's plan of salvation? Or, more personally, can our neighbors of other faiths be "saved" without becoming Christians? An extensive survey, published in 2008 by the Pew Forum on Religion and Public Life, found that "a majority of American Christians (52 percent) think that at least some non-Christian faiths can lead to eternal life." A substantial minority, however, believe that "mine is the one true faith," the only way of salvation; and the percentage of persons making such a claim has *increased* rather dramatically since 2002, especially among black Protestants and white evangelical Protestants.[3] Of course, sociological trends are no answer to a theological challenge; but such statistics make clear that this debate is, by no means, going away.

Even within churches involved in conciliar ecumenism, there is evident theological tension. The National Council of Churches' (NCC) policy statement "Interfaith Relations and the Churches," adopted in 1999, affirms and encourages interfaith dialogue and cooperation. But when it comes to the question "Can non-Christians be reconciled to God, and if so, how?" the statement reverts to the language of comparison: Some churches say this and others say that.[4]

2. See chapter 11 below.

3. "U.S. Religious Landscape Survey," at http://www.pewforum.org/Many-Americans
-Say-Other-Faiths-Can-Lead-to-Eternal-Life.aspx.

4. "Interfaith Relations and the Churches," par. 33, at http://www.ncccusa.org/interfaith/
ifr.html.

The current "position" of the World Council of Churches — first articulated at the 1989 Conference on World Mission and Evangelism in San Antonio, and since repeated in other reports — is not comparative but paradoxical: "We cannot point to any other way of salvation than Jesus Christ; at the same time, we cannot set limits to the saving power of God. . . . We appreciate the tension and do not attempt to resolve it."[5] A more recent document from the WCC (but one that has not received wide discussion in the churches), "Religious Plurality and Christian Self-Understanding," does go further by emphasizing the humility inherent in our finitude:

> . . . human limitations and limitations of language make it impossible for any community to have exhausted the mystery of salvation God offers to humankind. . . . [Thus we affirm] that salvation belongs to God, God only. We do not possess salvation; we participate in it. We do not offer salvation; we witness to it. We do not decide who would be saved; we leave it to the providence of God.[6]

This argument reminds me of a report I helped write for my denomination, the Disciples of Christ, in the late 1980s. With regard to God's ultimate treatment of people of other faiths, our theology commission said, in effect, Disciples are agnostic — we simply don't know. What we *know* is the grace of God we have experienced in Jesus Christ, an experience which gives us reason to *trust* that God will be merciful to others even as God has been merciful, beyond all deserving, to us.[7] To my ears, this sounded like a position most Christians could support. It was met, however, with vigorous opposition from persons claiming, among other things, that it undermined the church's evangelistic calling. As one of the milder responses put it, "It is difficult for people to give to Jesus the unreserved faith that he requires if they are thinking there are other ways to God besides him."[8]

Once again, we need to be clear about what is at issue and what is not.

---

5. Frederick R. Wilson, ed., *The San Antonio Report: Your Will Be Done, Mission in Christ's Way* (Geneva: WCC, 1990), pp. 32, 33.

6. "Religious Plurality and Christian Self-Understanding," par. 45, at http://www .oikoumene.org/fileadmin/files/wcc-main/documents/p2/fo_religiouspluralityandchristian self-understanding.pdf.

7. The theology commission report can be found in the 1990 *Year Book and Directory* of the Christian Church (Disciples of Christ), pp. 286-92. It is examined in Michael Kinnamon, "Jesus Christ and Salvation," *Lexington Theological Quarterly* 28 (Summer 1993): 125-37.

8. Quoted in Kinnamon, "Jesus Christ and Salvation," pp. 51-52.

Every text on this subject from the world and national councils affirms the importance — the necessity — of bearing bold witness, in word and deed, to the saving love of God in Christ. That is not in question. But neither, surely, is the need to proclaim the Good News with sensitivity, respect, and a willingness to listen as well as speak. The new document from the WCC, the Vatican, and the WEA echoes 1 Peter 3:15-16 when it says, "For Christians it is a privilege and joy to give an accounting for the hope that is within them, and to do so with gentleness and respect."[9] Conversion, as the text points out, is the work of the Holy Spirit. Our task is to tell what we have seen, and to do so in a way that is consistent with the gracious message we proclaim.

There is also broad convergence — not full agreement, but convergence — among Christians that God is *revealed* in other religions and, thus, that engagement with them affords real opportunity to experience God's presence, perhaps in ways that are new to us. We can explore the great divine Mystery with others to our own spiritual benefit.

The question of salvation, however, remains a challenge. And there are others related to it. Are we prepared to say, for example, that God wills the diversity of religions? Theologians such as Edward Schillebeeckx, Paul Knitter, and Peter Phan are already posing this question. In Knitter's words, "Is the manyness of religions a 'matter of fact' — that is, something we have to recognize but also overcome? Or is it instead a 'matter of principle' — a reality that we have to embrace because it is the way things are supposed to be?"[10]

I cannot overstate what a momentous challenge this is for the "classic" Christian theological tradition! We often point to human sexuality as the most profound, transformative theological challenge facing our churches; but seen in wider historical perspective, the interfaith challenge is far more radical.

2. The Ecumenical Challenge

The first challenge leads directly to the second: If the theological questions are not dealt with seriously and sensitively by the churches, then that failure will surely widen the already wide gap between the "dialoguers" and the "evangelizers," both of which claim the name of Christ. A good indication

9. "Christian Witness in a Multi-Religious World," A Basis for Christian Witness 1.
10. Paul Knitter, "The Religions Today: Their Challenge to the Ecumenical Movement," *Ecumenical Trends* 37 (March 2008): 7.

of this tension came at the 2005 Conference on World Mission and Evangelism, the first WCC-sponsored conference in decades to include a large number of representatives from evangelical and Pentecostal churches. Not coincidentally, interfaith relations did not figure in the conference theme or plenary presentations, and it was the subject of only one workshop.[11] It was a vivid reminder that, while new partners at the table can enrich conversation, they can also complicate it, a reminder that Christian unity and interfaith relations often stand in real tension.

If my seminary students over the years are any indication, many people in our pews now regard the search for Christian unity to be out-of-date, even exclusivist, seeing interfaith relations as the more important, and more exotic, alternative. I hope, however, that church leaders will continue to affirm that both are needed, even when one is more fun and exciting than the other.

I also hope that more liberal churches will not make the ecumenical task easier by dismissively condemning those who are suspicious of interfaith neighbors. I am thinking, for example, of a statement by the well-known historian of religions Wilfred Cantwell Smith that "the failure of Christians to affirm the saving action of God not just within other religious traditions but *through* them is blasphemy."[12] This kind of exclusive inclusivism avoids the ecumenical challenge by eliminating the possibility of learning from those who see the gospel through a different lens. Far preferable, in my judgment, is the position taken by Harvey Cox in an article for the *Christian Century.* "It is easier for me," writes Cox,

> to converse with universally minded Buddhists or Hindus than with fellow Christians who not only dismiss such people as pagans, but also want to dismiss me for not dismissing them as such. Still, I believe the critically important conversation among people of diverse faiths could founder and fail if we — the dialoguers — lose touch with our fellow believers who cluster on the particularist side. They remind us that without the radical particularity of the original revelation, we would have no faith to share. We remind them that without the universal dream, they falsify the message and diminish the scope of the original vision.[13]

11. See Jacques Matthey, ed., *Come Holy Spirit, Heal and Reconcile* (Geneva: WCC, 2008).

12. Quoted in Thomas J. J. Altizer, "Mission and Dialogue: 50 Years After Tambaram," *Christian Century* (April 6, 1988): 340.

13. Harvey Cox, "Many Mansions or One Way? The Crisis in Interfaith Dialogue," *Christian Century* (August 17-24, 1988): 735.

The necessity of interfaith relations should be a spur to ecumenical dialogue, forcing Christians to talk with one another about how they view the religious "other." And, conversely, progress in Christian unity should contribute to interfaith work by enabling our partners, who are often perplexed by the contradictory stands taken by Christians, to trust our commitments.

3. The Moral Challenge

The third challenge I have in mind is probably the toughest: the challenge of being both open to legitimate diversity and firmly opposed to those diversities, including some called "religious," that are demonic. Or as theologian Marjorie Hewitt Suchocki once put it, we must be able to distinguish between Jonestown and an Amish village.[14]

The very experience of religious and cultural diversity has led many persons — especially, I think, those in younger generations — to conclude that religious beliefs and moral values are a matter of personal preference. Live and let live. This attitude has the benefit of opening us to differences, but the question is whether it will stand the test of evil. If one belief is really as good as the next, then how do we say no to Qur'an-burning congregations or religious practices that demean women or advocates of religiously based terrorism with sufficient conviction? Saying yes to neighbors of another faith means saying no to those things that harm or diminish them. Otherwise, our very openness can mask what Herbert Marcuse called a "repressive tolerance" that allows racism or sexism or xenophobia to flourish in the name of diversity.[15]

All of this seems particularly important in an age when religion is being used to foster, justify, and intensify violence. Rabbi Jonathan Sacks makes

14. Marjorie Hewitt Suchocki, "In Search of Justice: Religious Pluralism from a Feminist Perspective," in John Hick and Paul F. Knitter, eds., *The Myth of Christian Uniqueness* (Maryknoll, N.Y.: Orbis Books, 1987), p. 160.

15. I had some of this in mind when, during my years as general secretary of the NCC, I declined invitations to church-sponsored dinners with Iranian President Ahmadinejad, and, instead, accepted invitations to speak at Jewish-sponsored rallies denouncing his hateful rhetoric that threatens Jews and Israel. Yes, I assured irritated Christian colleagues, I believe in eating with enemies. But, as Paul wrote to the church at Rome, "Let love be genuine; *hate* what is evil, hold fast to what is good" (Rom. 12:9). If I am to love all those whom God (the Universal Lover) loves, then I must oppose those ways of acting and speaking which threaten those whom God loves.

this point with great power in his wonderful book *The Dignity of Difference*. "We must," he writes, "withhold the robe of sanctity when it is sought as a cloak for violence and bloodshed. If faith is enlisted in the cause of war, there must be an equal and opposite counter-voice in the name of peace. If religion is not part of the solution, it will certainly be part of the problem."[16]

Discerning when to affirm and when to oppose is hard enough in cases where religion is linked to violence; but there are other cases where it is agonizingly complicated. For example, are certain forms of traditional Muslim practice regarding women (at least in certain cultures) to be accepted as religious diversity or denounced as violations of human rights? One of the most difficult discussions I witnessed during my decade as dean of Lexington Theological Seminary came when a local delegate to the U.N. Conference on Population and Development (Cairo, 1994), speaking at a seminary convocation, denounced female circumcision, what many call genital mutilation, as evil, as a practice that is wrong in every setting and should be universally eliminated — only to be denounced, in turn, by African students for her insensitivity to other cultures and religions. All of us, I suspect, would reject the caste system as inhumane, but how does that affect our relations with Brahmanic Hinduism? What are we prepared to say about religious-based rejection or support of homosexuality? Is this an issue on which it is appropriate to agree to disagree — or is something more fundamental at stake?

Notice how all of this profoundly complicates the ecumenical challenge. To put it baldly: Is Christian exclusivism a form of religion that other Christians must denounce because it threatens the neighbor? As I indicated earlier in my comment on the quotation from Wilfred Cantwell Smith, my general response is no. The idea that Christianity is a spiritually superior faith has grounding in parts of Scripture; and it is certainly possible to claim that insisting others follow Christ is the deepest expression of love. But, while there is not a *necessary* link between exclusivist theology and violence, there is surely a *possible* link between claiming that one's faith is superior and calling for aggression against those who do not accept it.

4. The Missional Challenge

In order to grasp this challenge fully, we need to start with a brief historical review. One of the most notable developments in ecumenical thought over

---

16. Jonathan Sacks, *The Dignity of Difference* (London: Continuum, 2002), p. 9.

the past half century is the claim, now widely embraced, that mission is, most essentially, *missio Dei* — the mission of God. Christians used to talk about the churches' *missions;* now we speak more of God's *mission* in which the church is privileged to participate. Under the old paradigm, mission was practically synonymous with evangelism, with planting more churches and bringing more people to knowledge and love of Christ. The concept of *missio Dei* widens the understanding of mission to include God's whole work of healing and reconciliation. Christians are still called to witness to Christ, but we do so not just through proclamation but through service, advocacy for justice, and peacemaking.

The challenge of this era is whether we can and must go further — to affirm that mission, which used to be aimed *at* interfaith neighbors, must now be done *with* them. I take it that at-least-occasional cooperation is no longer at issue. The "Christian Witness" text, co-authored by evangelical Christians, urges churches and councils of churches to "cooperate with other religious communities, engaging in interreligious advocacy towards justice and the common good, and, wherever possible, standing together in solidarity with people who are in situations of conflict."[17] It makes no sense to talk about the *Christian* response to climate change or global poverty! The issues are simply too big to be dealt with apart from other communities of faith.

But, and here is where things get more challenging, if God's mission calls us to protect the environment and act on behalf of the poor, and if such ministry needs to be done in collaboration with interfaith partners, then it follows that interfaith relations are essential for Christian mission. It is not only expedient to work with others; it is an act of faithfulness to do so. And if that is true, then persons of other faiths should be more than "guests" at Christian assemblies. They should be present as full participants in the mission of the church.

5. The Identity Challenge

The identity challenge is, to some extent, a summary of the first four. To put it in the form of a question, How does interfaith encounter affect the way we understand ourselves — our identity — as followers of Christ?

For much of human history, people have defined themselves, often in religious terms, over against those who are "other." *We* are not *them*! This is

---

17. "Christian Witness in a Multi-Religious World," Recommendation 4.

evident today in what is loosely called "fundamentalism" — which, as I see it, is the religious expression of the anxiety that so pervades contemporary society. Fundamentalist religion assumes scarcity: If we are right, they must be wrong. If we are saved, they must be lost. Fundamentalist communities draw lines to keep their identity secure by keeping others out.

Recent ecumenical documents, however, have turned this approach to identity on its head by emphasizing the biblical theme of hospitality. The WCC's "Religious Plurality and Christian Self-Understanding," for example, suggests that hospitality, welcoming the stranger, is not simply a practice but an identity. Who are we? We are those who welcome others, just as Abraham welcomed angels by the oaks of Mamre (Gen. 18:1-8; Heb. 13:1-2), just as God has welcomed us in Christ (Rom. 15:7). Early Christians, in the words of a study booklet from the NCC, "practiced hospitality not as a tactic to increase membership, but because it was truly at the heart of their identity. . . . It was in their acts of hospitality that the gospel shone brightly."[18]

Seen from this perspective, hospitality toward people of other faiths is not relativism or a betrayal of Christian mission; it is an expression of Christ's call to love our neighbors as ourselves and our truest witness to the grace we have experienced in him. Such hospitality is also not a matter of altruism. The "stranger" from another religion can challenge our pet assumptions, forcing us to think about God more deeply — which is why so many of the spiritual giants of our age have stressed the importance of welcoming others. No one, writes Thomas Merton, knows that the stranger he meets is not the one who has some providential or prophetic message to utter.[19]

It is not surprising, then, that the plenary discussion on interfaith relations at the WCC's 2006 assembly in Porto Alegre, Brazil, took place under the heading "Christian Identity and Religious Plurality." To be honest, however, the challenge posed by this era of interreligious engagement is more radical than ecumenical conferences have yet acknowledged. I think, for example, of the work of Catholic theologian John Dunne, who argues that being a person of faith in our time involves "passing over" from one religion to another and back again, bearing new insight.[20] Or the testimony offered by the eminent scholar Raimon Panikkar. "I was brought up in the Catholic religion by my Spanish mother," he told an interviewer in the *Christian Century,*

---

18. "The Identity Challenge," p. 5, at http://www.ncccusa.org/interfaith/IFRidentity.pdf.
19. Accessed at http://www.octanecreative.com/merton/quotes.html.
20. See John S. Dunne, *The Way of All the Earth* (New York: Macmillan, 1972).

but I never stopped trying to be united with the tolerant and generous religion of my father and my Hindu ancestors. This does not make me a cultural or religious "half-caste," however. Christ was not half man and half God, but fully man and fully God. In the same way, I consider myself 100 percent Hindu and Indian, and 100 percent Catholic and Spanish. How is that possible? By living religion as an experience rather than as an ideology.[21]

I also think of Roy Sano, a much-beloved bishop (now retired) in the United Methodist Church. "Christians used to ask us Asians," writes Sano, "how can you be Christians when you are still Buddhist? Christians of Asian heritage are now reversing the question: 'How do you expect us to be Christian without being Buddhist?'"[22] This is not a matter of joining a Buddhist community, but of drawing deeply and openly from a cultural heritage that has been decisively shaped by a Buddhist ethos.

Such challenge to traditional understandings of Christian identity will surely multiply in the coming years. And, as we have seen, this is only one of the challenges, stemming from interfaith encounter, that Christians will need to face in the future — and even now.

21. "Eruption of Truth: An Interview with Raimon Panikkar," *Christian Century* (August 16-23, 2000): 834.

22. Roy Sano, "'Holy Moments' at Canberra," *Christianity and Crisis* 51 (July 15, 1991): 228.

CHAPTER 11

How Can We Deal with the Tough Issues in Jewish-Christian Relations?

with a response by Rabbi Steve Gutow[1]

The history of relations between Christians and Jews is marked by nearly continuous, often murderous, animosity and estrangement, for which Christians bear the lion's share of responsibility. Thus, the astonishing improvement in this relationship over the past half century, particularly in the United States, is surely cause for great thanksgiving!

There are at least two reasons for this positive change. First, the Holocaust forced Christians to face their culpability for the anti-Semitism that laid the groundwork for that monstrous horror; and this, in turn, has increased Christian sensitivity to the persistence of anti-Jewish attitudes and actions. Second, Christians and Jews now live side by side in the pluralistic societies of Europe and North America; and the resulting personal familiarity has prompted theological reassessment of the relationship.

The pivotal document in this process of reassessment was the "Declaration on the Relation of the Church to Non-Christian Religions" *(Nostra Aetate),* issued by the Second Vatican Council in 1965. The Roman Catholic Church, in the words of the text, "deplores all hatred, persecutions, displays of anti-Semitism leveled at any time or from any source against the Jews." The declaration explicitly affirms "the spiritual ties which link the people of the new covenant to the stock of Abraham," encourages further mutual

---

1. Rabbi Steve Gutow is president and chief executive officer of the Jewish Council for Public Affairs, and a leading voice in the American Jewish community in shaping public policy.

understanding among those who share this heritage, and rejects the charge that the Jews are responsible for the death of Jesus.[2]

Major statements followed, especially during the decade of the 1980s, from the World Council of Churches, a number of European Protestant communions, and nearly all of the mainline churches in the United States.[3] While they differ in emphasis and format, these statements share the following themes:

1. All of them repent of the church's complicity in the persecution of the Jewish people, repudiate anti-Semitism in all its forms, and state a commitment to oppose anti-Jewish attitudes in church and society.

2. The documents reject the tendency, so prevalent in the history of the church, to caricature or stereotype Jews and Judaism and affirm the need for Christians to be better acquainted with the life of the Jewish people, past and present.

3. They clearly affirm the importance of Judaism for a true understanding of Christian faith; indeed, most of these churches now acknowledge that Christian teachings about God's redemptive love are unintelligible apart from the story of Israel's election.

4. The statements generally claim that Jews and Christians bear a common responsibility, set forth clearly by the Hebrew prophets, to promote justice and peace — that they are partners in what the Jewish tradition calls *tikkun olam,* the "repairing of creation."

5. Perhaps most significantly, these churches affirm God's continuing covenantal relationship with the Jewish people, and, correspondingly, repudiate the notion that the church has replaced or "superseded" Israel in God's favor. There is not agreement on whether Christians have a mission to the Jews (whether it is ever appropriate to seek their conversion), but there is agreement that dialogue is an appropriate form of relationship.

These are by no means insignificant affirmations. They have contributed to a tremendous burst of local and national cooperation. Yet, over the past two decades, these gains have been increasingly threatened by profound

2. *Nostra Aetate,* par. 4, at http://www.vatican.va/archive/hist_councils/ii_vatican_council/documents/vat-ii_decl_19651028_nostra-aetate_en.html.

3. Several of these statements can be found in *The Theology of the Churches and the Jewish People: Statements by the World Council of Churches and Its Member Churches* (Geneva: WCC, 1988) and on the websites of U.S. mainline denominations. For an expanded version of these points, see Michael Kinnamon, "Signs of Hope in Jewish-Christian Relations," in Clark W. Williamson, ed., *The Church and the Jewish People* (St. Louis: Christian Board of Publications, 1994), pp. 65-72.

disagreements regarding policies and actions of the Israeli government and its conflict with the Palestinians.

Guidelines for Maintaining Relationship

During my years with the National Council of Churches (NCC), my colleagues and I had close working relationships with Jewish organizations, especially the Jewish Council for Public Affairs (JCPA) and the Religious Action Center of the Union for Reform Judaism. Public witness on such matters as environmental protection and poverty reduction was nearly always done with these Jewish partners. At the same time, however, the Jewish-Christian dialogue carried out through the NCC's Interfaith Relations Commission all but collapsed because of differences over the Israeli-Palestinian conflict. The churches that make up the NCC, many of which have roots and/or mission partners in the Middle East, have called for an end to Israeli occupation of land captured during the 1967 war and have condemned the expansion of Israeli settlements, the building of a separation barrier on occupied land, and the extensive system of roadblocks and checkpoints that separates Palestinian workers from their jobs, farmers from their fields, children from their schools, patients from hospitals, and worshipers from holy places.[4] Needless to say, our Jewish colleagues have a different perspective, often defending Israeli policy (though not all of its applications) as necessary for the country's security in the face of Palestinian terrorism, and arguing that Palestinian rejection of Israeli peace offers is a major reason for the continued occupation.

As NCC general secretary, I was extremely fortunate — I will dare say blessed — to have a close personal friend, Rabbi Steve Gutow, as my counterpart at the JCPA. In addition to sharing work on poverty, torture, climate change, and discrimination, Rabbi Gutow and I tried to address the tension outlined above. Are there things that Christians and Jews can do to build up the relationship, even when we do not see eye to eye on an issue of great consequence? Are there ways to find common ground without sacrificing the integrity of our concerns? We believe the answer to these questions is yes.

---

4. See "Reaffirmation of Our Commitments to Peace in the Middle East in Light of the 1980 Middle East Policy Statement," received by the General Assembly of the National Council of Churches and Church World Service in November 2007, at www.ncccusa.org/pdfs/reaffirmationMEpolicy110707.pdf.

In what follows, I will name nine lessons that I learned from this experience, nine guidelines for maintaining relationship while dealing with tough issues. And I have invited Rabbi Gutow to respond.

1. *Cultivate personal relationships* because there is simply no substitute for knowing one another as friends. Friends try to understand one another when faced with disagreement. Friends recognize that differences on public issues may well be grounded in moral/religious convictions and are not simply "opinions." Friends don't assume ulterior motives but trust one another to act and speak with integrity. Friends seek the advice of one another on matters of common concern, and they dare to speak honestly when things get tense.

I vividly recall the evening Steve called me at home to say, "Your colleagues are acting badly!" A Christian participant in the official dialogue involving our organizations had sent a letter to the JCPA that could be read as questioning the integrity of one of Steve's co-workers. Steve was prepared to respond with a sharply worded letter of his own, which he read to me (I think) so I could talk him out of it. This I did, which prevented further escalation of the tension. But Steve had also effectively communicated his concern and motivated me to speak with the author of the original letter. And thus he stood up for his colleague. Never underestimate the importance of friendship!

2. *Be sensitive to the fears and pressures that weigh on the other.* Whether seen as a place of refuge or as an expression of ancient hope, modern Israel is of great importance to most Jews, including those living in the United States. For many, including Steve, it is integral to their self-understanding as Jews. This means that insufficient regard for Israel's welfare, especially at a time when it seems threatened by surrounding countries, is incompatible with genuine concern for the Jewish community. I do hope that Christians will speak out on behalf of Palestinians' rights and a viable, independent Palestinian state, which may well mean criticism of policies and actions of the Israeli government. If, however, we are sensitive to the fears and commitments of Jewish neighbors, then such criticism must be set within an affirmation of Israel's right to exist in peace and security. Prior to the fighting in Gaza in 2009, I, in my role as NCC general secretary, should have spoken out against the missile attacks on Israeli towns — and the fact that I didn't undermined my credibility with Jewish leaders once the attack on Gaza began.

One of the things we need to be sensitive to is the fact that our partners in this country have co-religionists in other places to whom they must listen. I have had people ask me why the churches are so exercised on behalf of

Palestinians when "Christians don't have a dog in that fight." But, of course, that is not true. Just as American Jews are attentive to the fears of Jews in Haifa and Tel Aviv, so American Christians are (increasingly) attentive to the fears of Christians in Bethlehem and Ramallah — including the alarmingly high level of emigration that is diminishing their community.[5] There are various reasons why the percentage of Christians in the Palestinian territories has fallen so dramatically in recent decades, but a major factor is the hardship associated with the occupation and ongoing conflict. And, as a result, churches in the West Bank are in danger of becoming more like museums for others to visit than vital, contemporary communities of faith. Jewish friends like Steve appreciate this concern and recognize its importance for their Christian partners.

3. *Be present when the other requests it or is in need.* Whenever Iranian President Mahmoud Ahmadinejad came to New York for the opening session of the United Nations General Assembly, I would be asked by Steve to speak at public events protesting Ahmadinejad's hateful rhetoric regarding Jews and Israel. Some Christian colleagues would counsel a different course of action, inviting me to join them at a dinner where the Iranian leader would speak and receive questions. I believe in the importance of dialogue with enemies, but I always declined this invitation and accepted Steve's because I know that the Jewish community regards Iran as the greatest threat to Israel's existence. My presence *at that moment* spoke loudly to Steve and other Jewish leaders about the importance I give to our relationship.

In the same way, it mattered greatly to me that, on five occasions, Steve accompanied me for conversations with the Israeli ambassador to the United States, and that he joined in my protest of Israeli policies and practices that negatively affect Palestinians, including Palestinian Christians.[6] To take another example, in 2010, as part of the increased security surrounding Passover, the Israeli government blocked access of Palestinian Christians to Easter celebrations in the Old City of Jerusalem. I raised the issue with Steve and Rabbi David Saperstein of the Religious Action Center, both of

5. See, e.g., "The Sabeel Survey on Palestinian Christians in the West Bank and Israel," Summer 2006, at http://www.sabeel.org/datadir/en-events/ev131/files/the%20sabeel%20survey%20-%20english%202008.pdf.

6. The issues we raised were the revocation of identity cards of Palestinians returning home from study or work abroad (thus denying them residence rights), the delay in issuing building permits for Palestinians or international organizations working in Palestinian areas, and the splitting of Palestinian families when husband and wife have different identity papers.

whom interceded with the ambassador — and checkpoints were, at least partially, opened.

These are not simply instances of *quid pro quo;* Steve might well speak out on behalf of Palestinians without my invitation, even as I would care about Israel's security without his encouragement. But they do underscore the mutual benefit of taking seriously what the other takes seriously, of being actively present when it matters greatly to the other. We can stay together through tough times if we have stood by one another in other times.

In 2002, at the height of the second Intifada and following several suicide bombings in Israeli cities, I was invited to speak at a "Stand with Israel" rally in St. Louis, Missouri, where I was then teaching — which I did, despite some discouragement from Christian friends. "Standing with Israel," I said in my remarks, "does not mean standing against the Palestinian people and their aspirations for peace and security; but it does mean saying 'No!' to suicide bombing and other acts of terror against civilians. . . . The time when friends stand with friends is not simply when it is easy to do so, but precisely when it is not. And so I say to my colleagues in the church, *now* is that time." Jewish friends in St. Louis still tell me that they listen more carefully to my support for Palestinian rights because I was present when they had need in 2002.

4. *Keep the other informed of developments that could be problematic.* In 2009, a group of leading Palestinian Christians issued what is widely known as the Kairos Palestine document, "a word of faith, hope, and love from the heart of Palestinian suffering."[7] This text, which stands in the tradition of similar documents from such places as South Africa and Central America, contends that Israeli occupation of land in which Palestinians have deep roots "is a sin against God and humanity because it deprives the Palestinians of their basic human rights, bestowed by God." The authors argue that, despite all appearances, this is a "kairos" moment (i.e., a time filled with the possibility of substantive change), when churches, including those in the United States, are called to speak and act prophetically, to resist the occupation in courageous but peaceful ways.

Kairos Palestine was vigorously attacked by American Jewish organizations for echoing the discredited language of supersessionism (the belief that the church has replaced Israel as the people of God) — a real stretch, in my reading of the document — and for skating too lightly over the history of Arab violence against Israel — a far more valid critique. The Central

---

7. The Palestinian Kairos document can be accessed at http://www.kairospalestine.ps/sites/default/Documents/English.pdf.

Conference of American Rabbis (CCAR), part of the Reform movement of American Judaism, went so far as to say that it "would require serious reflection before continuing our common cause with any church body or organization that endorses . . . Kairos"[8] — the kind of ultimatum language that, in my judgment, undercuts the half century of rapprochement.

Soon after the release of Kairos Palestine, the NCC was urged from various quarters to commend the document for study in its member churches and to provide a study guide for that purpose. I authorized the development of such a guide;[9] but I also asked Steve to read a draft of it and to suggest a question that would raise Jewish concerns (with a link to the CCAR response). It was a way of affirming what I, personally, find to be a constructive, challenging theological statement, while also keeping Jewish colleagues fully informed.

In May 2010, Israeli commandos boarded a flotilla of ships that was intent on breaking the Israeli blockade of the Gaza Strip. Some activists on the ships fought back, and nine were killed by commandos. My response reflected what I was hearing from NCC member churches: "The National Council of Churches has strongly supported Israel's right to exist with peace and security, but this attack on an aid convoy contributes to neither. In fact, it undermines Israel's standing in the community of nations." The council also identified itself with the call of Churches for Middle East Peace to end the blockade against Gaza. But as we prepared the press release, I notified Steve so that he would not be caught off guard. Our commitment to positive relations between Christians and Jews does not mean we refrain from saying what each thinks must be said about contemporary events; but it does mean we keep the other informed, especially when things we say could be problematic.[10]

8. The CCAR response is at http://www.jcrelations.net/Resolution_on_the_2009_Kairos_Document.3288.0.html?L=9.

9. "Kairos Palestine: 'A Moment of Truth': A Summary and Guide for Further Study," at www.ncccusa.org/pdfs/kairosstudyguide.pdf.

10. After the initial draft of this chapter was written, the tension between U.S. churches and American Jewish organizations grew even more intense when Christian leaders, including my interim successor at the NCC, sent a letter to Congress (October 2012), asking for an investigation into possible violations by Israel of the U.S. Foreign Assistance Act. The letter suggested that Israel engages in a consistent pattern of human rights violations and other actions that undermine prospects for peace, and that U.S. law prohibits assistance when this is the case. The Christian leaders acknowledged that Israel faces real security threats and has a right to protect its citizens, but maintained that "continued U.S. military assistance to Israel — offered without conditions or accountability — will only serve to sustain the status quo and

5. *Refrain, if at all possible, from expressing convictions in ways that the other could find offensive.* Or, to put it positively, speak in ways that are intended to build up the relationship. Both Christians and Jews (generally) affirm that all governments stand under the judgment of the God of history; and that it is, therefore, appropriate to criticize any government according to the norms of justice set forth in our religious traditions. I have discovered, however, that criticisms of Israel can ring decidedly false in Jewish ears unless Christians (a) are critical of our own anti-Jewish past, (b) stand publicly with Jews when they are threatened by new outbreaks of anti-Semitism, and (c) are also critical of other governments, including that of the U.S., when *they* violate basic rights. Conversely, if criticism is offered in this spirit, then it should not be labeled "anti-Israel," let alone "anti-Semitic," because that, too, is offensive and unproductive.

I confess that the NCC has surely made statements — likely, many of them — that troubled our Jewish partners; but for purposes of this chapter, I will name two examples from my time at the council that go in the other direction. One was a JCPA fundraising letter that urged potential donors "to stand up for Israel in the face of divestment and other anti-Israel efforts such as those posed by Iran and Hezbollah." Whatever one thinks of policies of divestment (about which I will say more in a moment), it is offensive to link, even implicitly, churches that, after anguished debate, have adopted

---

Israel's military occupation of Palestinian territories." Jewish leaders, including Steve Gutow, responded with outrage — accusing the church leaders, in Steve's words, of participating in a "one-sided anti-Israel campaign" that overlooked the mistreatment of Christians in other Middle Eastern countries and ignored Palestinian culpability in the cycle of violence. They subsequently cancelled their involvement in a long-planned Christian-Jewish Roundtable, calling instead for a meeting of the heads of the churches and Jewish organizations in order to "determine a more positive path forward for our communities." The Jewish leaders also objected that they were not consulted, or even notified, in advance of the letter's release — which underscores the importance of the fourth guideline offered in this chapter. Guideline 2, however, also comes to mind. The Christian leaders surely know how important U.S. support for Israel is in the eyes of the U.S. Jewish community; but I am not sure that the Jewish community fully appreciates the pressure American churches feel from their Middle East partners to help break the current stalemate that so impoverishes the lives of Palestinians, including Christians. At the same time, guideline 3 is clearly applicable. Even if Christians feel compelled to take such a step as calling for investigation of U.S. assistance to Israel, the Jewish-Christian relationship would be less threatened if they also spoke out forcefully and consistently against rocket attacks on Israeli towns. The letter to Congress can be accessed at www.pcusa.org/news/2012/10/5/religious-leaders-ask-congress-condition-israel-mi/. Jewish responses, including quotations from Rabbi Gutow, are at engage.jewishpublicaffairs.org/blog/comments.jsp?blog_entry_KEY=6599.

such policies with the overt hostility of Iran and Hezbollah. Because of my relationship with Steve, I was able to express this concern of the churches directly, rather than allowing it to fester.

In the same way, I objected to language added to the JCPA Policy Compendium that, in my judgment and that of several Christian colleagues, criticized mainline Protestant churches for things they don't actually do (e.g., blame Israel alone for the conflict) and failed to acknowledge differences among them. Steve took these concerns seriously and, with considerable difficulty, had the policy amended to emphasize hopes for the future rather than rebukes for the past. Such sensitivity to the impact of language helps preserve positive relations even in the midst of tension and disagreement.

The question of whether to use economic leverage in an attempt to influence Israeli policy — frequently referred to as BDS: boycott, divestment, sanctions — is perhaps the most troubling current issue for the relationship between Jews and Christians. Two NCC member churches, as well as the World Council of Churches, have adopted resolutions initiating or calling for divestment from companies that contribute to the Israeli occupation. Other NCC-related churches have explicitly rejected such resolutions.

I, personally, have commended policies of *in*vestment in Palestinian enterprises, coupled with an increase in U.S. assistance to the Palestinian Authority, in part because I know that talk of BDS, and certainly any comparison to the apartheid regime in South Africa, ends the conversation with Jewish partners. And I believe that the churches have more actual effect on Israeli policy by way of friends in the U.S. Jewish community than by way of direct economic action.

6. *Act together whenever possible on a common agenda.* Even when tensions over the Middle East conflict were particularly acute, there was much that the NCC and the JCPA could do together — indeed, much that we *needed* to do together in order to fulfill the advocacy mandates authorized by our governing bodies. During my four years at the council, Steve and I collaborated directly on poverty relief — demanding, for example, that the poor be taken into account in legislative debates over the budget — through a program titled "Fighting Poverty with Faith"; promoted environmental protection and called attention to the looming dangers of climate change through our participation in the National Religious Partnership on the Environment; opposed Islamophobia and other expressions of religious discrimination through a program called "Shoulder to Shoulder," initiated by the Islamic Society of North America (ISNA); called for genuine health care reform that would give special attention to the poorest and sickest in society;

and expressed strong opposition to torture, especially that perpetrated by the U.S. in recent years, through common participation in the National Religious Campaign Against Torture. And this is a very incomplete list.[11]

There is an obvious, but still important, distinction between interfaith relations and interfaith dialogue. The latter is sustained conversation aimed at sharing the communities' faith-based perspectives on a common topic in order to arrive at deeper mutual understanding. By interfaith relations, I take it, we mean various forms of life together, including shared action for justice, through which persons of faith and their communities gain greater appreciation for one another. Interfaith dialogue is of real significance and can, at times, provide a foundation for broader interfaith collaboration; but acting together can also help dialogues persevere when the going gets tough.

7. *Avoid generalizations about the other.* Talk of *the* Jewish position or *the* Christian position on just about any subject should make us all laugh out loud! I am actually astonished at what the NCC churches can say together, including about the Middle East; but it is still best to avoid generalizations with a constituency that ranges from the Greek Orthodox to the Quakers. And the same is true for the JCPA, an umbrella that covers Reform, Reconstructionist, Conservative, and Orthodox Jewish organizations. American Jews from any of these traditions are often reluctant to criticize Israel publicly for fear of aiding its enemies; but there is, in fact, real diversity on the Israeli-Palestinian conflict within American Jewry — and, if my experience is any indication, considerable sympathy for ordinary Palestinians. I suspect that many Jews in this country agree with the famous Jewish philosopher Martin Buber that true lovers of Israel must uphold justice for other inhabitants of the land — which is a direct challenge to the stereotype, held by many Christians, of unquestioning Jewish support for Israeli actions. But no statement will express the mind of the whole community.

The basic principle toward which I am pointing, applicable to any dialogue or relationship, is to allow others to define themselves — to describe and witness to their faith in their own terms. Generalizations are usually a form of stereotyping, a way of lumping persons of another religious community into a one-size-fits-all box that inhibits real conversation.

8. *Act and speak with integrity.* Tempting as it sometimes is, it would never do for me to say one thing to Palestinian Christians and another to

---

11. There is no doubt that my own reluctance, while at the NCC, to support such initiatives as economic boycott and divestment was driven, at least in part, by the knowledge that this would make cooperation on social issues more difficult.

American Jews. Real trust is based on the conviction that the partner is consistent, speaking and acting in the same way in different settings.

Steve and I would not talk in terms of holding one another accountable, but, in fact, we did so by making joint public presentations. In this way, we "overheard" one another speaking to different audiences — Jewish, Christian, interfaith — and knew that the other's message, while appropriately adapted to various settings, was fundamentally consistent. These times were confirmations of the integrity on which our relationship was built.

9. *Pray together for God's guidance in times when differences seem irreconcilable.* No one wishes for difficult times or for moments of real disagreement between friends. And it is never appropriate to speak of silver linings when people are hurting. But Steve and I have acknowledged to one another that such times, since we can't take pride in what *we* accomplish, can drive us back to the spiritual heart of our traditions.

Prayer shifts the focus beyond ourselves to the Holy One who is infinitely more than our positions and strategies. It reminds us of our common heritage as children of one Creator and our common calling to care for every neighbor, not just for those who belong to "us." Prayer for and with the other is not a substitute for practical acts of solidarity and shared service; rather it mobilizes our imagination and will to act as God would have us act. Prayer is not a religious way of stifling protest, but is itself a profound protest against the reduction of life to self-interested projects and human-sized conflicts.

In January 2009, as Palestinian rockets were fired at Israeli cities and Israel's army responded with an assault on militants in the Gaza Strip, Steve and I acknowledged that we had very different views of this conflict and how to end it, views that were expressed through the channels of the JCPA and the NCC. But what could we, should we, say together? The answer was a prayer, authored jointly by the two of us and Dr. Sayeed Sayyid, a leader in ISNA. Through it we affirmed that we belong to one another, even when human differences seem irreconcilable:

Dear Lover of humanity and all creation, we come to you because we trust in your power and take comfort in your compassion.

Our world is in chaos. Your children suffer greatly in Afghanistan and Darfur, Burma, the Congo, and Sri Lanka — and the Middle East is a place of soul-wrenching strife. With no end in sight and no reason for easy hope, You are the One to whom we turn.

Strengthen us, Merciful God, to act and to know that our acting matters: raising awareness at home of suffering in distant places, advocating

for peace instead of violence, bringing together those who have been estranged, trying, ourselves, to see the world as others see it.

Fill us, we pray, with the vision of a time when children are not killed
in war, and in which the neighbor's well-being is a first priority.

We have not always agreed on decisions involving war and peace,
but we do agree that You are on the side of those who suffer, and that
peacemaking is our ultimate vocation. We pray in different ways and languages, but we each long to hear Your voice and to discern the way You
wish us to travel.

Blessed are You, Holy One! May Your will for peace prevail! Amen.

Response from Rabbi Steve Gutow

Michael and I have developed a rich personal friendship that has given us
the will to learn from each other and to do the collaborative actions that
Michael mentions above. We have attempted to practice the nine principles
he names, working and praying together even when we have differed on
matters related to the Israeli-Palestinian conflict. What we have also learned
is that, when we look, we can find ways to support each other, not needing
to make every difference, even with regard to war and peace in the world, a
war between the two of us.

What, for me, is the core concern in the struggle for peace between Israelis and Palestinians? I, and probably the majority of Jews in America, do
not see the conflict as driven primarily by policies of the Israeli government.
I do have questions about those policies, particularly the settlement policies,
but the settlements are far from the crux of the problem. If there were no
settlements at all, or if the settlement growth were stopped in its tracks, there
would still be difficult challenges for the parties on the path to peace.

In my view, the Palestinians have never provided a clear sense that they
support a unified plan to live on the West Bank and Gaza in peace with an independent and Jewish Israel, and have thereby pushed Israel toward tougher
security policies. After the 1967 war, when Israel for clearly defensive reasons
captured the West Bank and Gaza from Jordan and Egypt, it took twenty
years for the Palestine Liberation Organization to renounce the parts of its
charter calling for an end to the Jewish state. After the Oslo Accord of 1993,
which failed for a host of reasons not solely attributable to either party, the
Palestinian Authority literally walked away from two peace offers made by

Israel. And the Palestinian Authority is the party of the Palestinian people most open to peace! The powerful and fundamentalist Muslim Hamas party still contends that any peace agreement with Israel is simply a respite from war until the Palestinians are strong enough to conquer all of Israel.

All of this has helped me understand why the Israeli government tilts so far toward policies of security rather than toward the compromises and sacrifices necessary for peace. Imagine how Americans would react in a similar situation. If a democratic country does not believe that the other side truly wants to work for peace, why should or would the citizens of that country take such a risk? It is with this viewpoint in mind that I offer my response.

I agree with Michael's rendition of the nine principles we both hold dear. I have come to believe, however, that three more principles should be added somewhere in the list — leaving "pray together for God's guidance" as the most important and culminating principle:

1. *Be willing to modify positions or statements when evidence warrants such a change.* Many Jews have grown up with the false belief that Arab Christians and Muslims are treated very well, as equal to Israeli Jews, in Israel proper. Time has shown that this belief is just not true. Some of the necessities of life — including education, water rights, and economic aid — have not been fairly distributed by Israel to its many municipalities, and the Arab population suffers under these unfair conditions. Israel has made strides toward removing such injustice, but still has much to do. The main players in the American Jewish community are also committed to changing this situation, but it is very hard for some American Jews to admit that these disparities ever existed or still exist — and this inhibits closer relations.

On the other side of the equation, I discovered (as did many Christians and Jews) through a JCPA demographic study,[12] that one of the totemic arguments against Israeli control of the West Bank — that the Palestinian Christian population has decreased dramatically under Israeli rule — simply does not stand up to scrutiny. Although the percentage of Christians has declined significantly during Israel's control of the Palestinian territories, the actual number of Christians, contrary to what we often hear, has risen under Israeli hegemony, according to our study. By contrast, the Christian population decreased during the twenty years of Jordanian rule prior to the 1967 war. I want to state clearly that, to the best of my knowledge, neither

12. "JCPA Background Paper: The Palestinian Christian Population," at https://org2 .democracyinaction.org/o/5145/images/JCPA%20Background%20Paper%20on%20Palestinian %20Christians%207%202.pdf.

Michael nor the National Council of Churches has claimed in public statements that the actual number of Christians in the West Bank has diminished
since 1967; but, as the JCPA study shows, others certainly have.

What I learned from our study and the subsequent Christian response
was that Palestinian Christians and their American supporters — some of
them, at any rate — not only held up falsity as fact, but even when it became clear that their facts were false did not acknowledge that they had
been wrong or mention that other factors help account for the decreasing
percentage of Christians: a far lower birthrate among Palestinian Christians
than among Palestinian Muslims and greater prosperity that allows them the
luxury of emigration. What also seems to be lost in this particular dialogue is
that the actual number of Christians, not just their percentage in the population, has fallen, and that Christians have been poorly treated in some Muslim
countries (where there is no significant Jewish presence) — all of which has
received far less attention in Christian public relations efforts. When totems
of a political ideology are shown to be false, it takes courage to admit it.

None of the above is to suggest that Israel does not have a long way to go
in improving its treatment of Palestinians, including Palestinian Christians.
It does! That is why I not only set up and joined Michael at meetings with
the Israeli ambassador to the United States, but have done much on my own
to promote just policies, including passage through checkpoints, attainment
of visas, and rights to land and water. It is simply that I think we should add
this additional principle. Admitting a new truth when the old "truth" is no
longer valid is a difficult but essential quality of a good relationship.

2. *Be willing to challenge members of your own faith community when
they take a position you believe to be wrong.* Michael has spoken fairly about
both sides of the conflict to members of the Christian community, even
when his speaking might be seen as criticism of Christian allies. When
Michael spoke out against the hateful rhetoric of President Ahmadinejad,
during the Iranian leader's visits to the United Nations, he was not only being
sensitive to the concerns of Jewish friends but also standing up to many of
his Christian brothers and sisters who wanted to treat Ahmadinejad as an
important and respected leader on the world stage who should be engaged
in reasoned debate.

3. *Bend over backward to understand both sides of an issue when you
know your inclinations fall strongly in one direction or the other.* One such
issue is the efficacy of the wall, or security barrier, that Israel built to protect
its citizens. The wall does seem to have deterred suicide bombings. That
does not mean, however, that the wall is the only solution to that problem or

deny that in places the barrier trespasses on Palestinian property. Dialogue partners will acknowledge both points.

Another example is the flotilla that tried to break through the Israeli blockade of Gaza. The Israeli efforts to stop it wound up causing the deaths of nine Palestinian supporters. International law says that any country, if fearful that weapons that could be used to attack it are being transported into it, has the right to prevent those weapons from reaching their destination. Whether or not Israel stopped the boat in the best, most humane way is an important question, but the one-sided rhetoric used by many who oppose Israel made genuine discussion of Israel's methods nearly impossible. If the starting point is that the Israelis were inhumane and murderous, the conversation will stop before a reasonable understanding can be reached.

The Kairos document Michael mentions above is another case in point. Michael suggests that, from his viewpoint and that of Palestinian Christians, the document is "a word of faith, hope, and love from the heart of Palestinian suffering." But for me and many Jewish leaders, the document is a demagogic treatise, painting the Palestinian cause as purely righteous, never mentioning specific Palestinian infractions. Worse, the document refers to Israel's occupation of the West Bank as "evil," giving the impression that Israel's participation in the occupation is evil — a word that is guaranteed to stop dialogue before it begins. In fact, it defies my imagination that one can call the actions of the other evil (with its implication of intense theological abomination) and then expect the other to engage in rational conversation! Perhaps the settlement policy can be described as immoral and a detriment to peace, but that is a far cry from calling it evil.

While not all will agree, I am convinced that there are defensible reasons why Israel continues to maintain control of Palestinian territories. Reading the Kairos document, one might think that all belligerence is the fault of Israel, since there is no mention of the unwillingness of Palestinian leaders to act on behalf of peace. Dialogue partners need to acknowledge the complexity and ambiguity of such issues.

What does all this mean to me? Relations between the Jewish community and the mainstream Christian churches should start from the realization that we have many areas of common work. As I see it, we are well advised to focus on such issues as support for the poor and not allow differences over the conflict to undermine such vital collaboration. In families, if there is any hope for peace in the house, family members discuss the good times without dwelling on the tensions and exasperations that often are also part of family relations.

Michael and I have spent a lot of time together. I was asked to read poetry at his wedding, an indication that we know a good bit about one another — including strengths and weaknesses. Our relationship is based on integrity, belief in G-d, and love for each other. We know that we do not agree on certain matters; but because our friendship comes from such a deep place, we have learned how best to differ, criticize, and work together. If I had to distill all that I've been saying, it would be this: Speak and listen in gentle ways that show the other respect; work on those things that build up the relationship and love for one another; and when you must disagree, know the heart and the story of the other. Finally, if you believe in G-d, think about how a loving G-d would engage in whatever you are doing or saying. And set everything in the context of prayer.

Afterword: The Gift of *Hevruta*

The initial draft of Steve's response to this chapter surfaced more disagreement, at least at first glance, than we had previously realized or anticipated. Steve felt that the chapter reflected, to some extent, positions that overlook real threats to Israel's survival. I felt that he had responded somewhat defensively, focusing on things that I didn't say or had touched on only lightly. What to do?

At this point Steve suggested that we engage in an ancient Jewish process of close textual study between friends, called *hevruta* (from the Hebrew word for friend, *haver*).[13] The process is both simple and profound: The friends take turns reading parts of the text aloud, offering immediate comments and questions, after which they discuss together: What does the text say? What does it mean? What does it mean to me?

Hevruta is a deliberately noncompetitive way of study rooted in the assumption that shared insights can deepen understanding and correct misapprehensions. Our experience confirmed that reading in the presence of the other changes the way the text is perceived. We were able to hear one another's concerns, see what words had triggered those concerns, and find common language that preserved the integrity of what both of us were trying to say. Thus, the final draft of this chapter not only speaks about interfaith dialogue, it is an example of it.

13. A helpful brief definition and guide to the process of *hevruta* can be found at www .mussarleadership.org/hevruta.html.

CHAPTER 12

Are Councils of Churches a Thing of the Past?

In one sense, the answer to the question posed by the title of this chapter is obviously no. Conciliarity, the impulse to gather in council in order to address issues of common concern, has been evident throughout the history of Christianity, beginning with the Council of Jerusalem recorded in Acts 15; thus, it would seem to belong to the essence of the church.

The English word "council" can be misleading, however, since it carries two distinct meanings. Other European languages generally have one term (in French, *concile*) for the authoritative gatherings of the ancient church (e.g., the Council of Nicea) or of some contemporary churches (e.g., the Second Vatican Council), and a second term *(conseil)* for the voluntary associations of still-separated churches (e.g., the World Council of Churches). The question asked by this chapter is whether councils of this latter sort — which, it is fair to say, have been the most widely recognized expressions of the modern ecumenical movement — have a future. Having sprung up in the early part of the twentieth century, are these councils now a thing of the past?

The question arises because, over the past generation, councils of churches have lost vitality or shut down altogether, not only in the United States but around the world. Nearly every council I have observed struggles to obtain adequate funding, with the result that concern for survival takes precedence over innovative thinking. And there are other challenges — including the need to expand membership beyond the "usual suspects" and the need for increased accountability of the member churches to one another and for their life as council — that are echoed by leaders of the World Council of Churches (WCC) and national councils of churches on every continent.

I have written extensively in other places about councils at the world and national levels.[1] In this chapter, therefore, I want to focus most of our attention on state and local councils of churches, asking what it will take for them to be part of the church's future, not just its past. It has been my privilege to meet with boards, assemblies, or other gatherings of councils in nearly every state, to observe (even participate in) their efforts to achieve institutional viability and missional coherence. In this chapter I want to share some of what I have learned and offer my own practical thoughts about renewal.

Common Themes

In one sense, it is difficult to generalize about state and local conciliar life since councils of churches are quite contextual — dependent on key individuals, with different histories, configurations of churches, and pressing issues. That said, there are still common themes that allow a council in one place to learn from those in other settings; and it is these themes on which I will concentrate. You will find no references in this chapter to specific councils, since this is not intended to be a survey or comprehensive study. Rather, what follows are reflections, rooted in experience, of someone who cares deeply about local ecumenism and hopes to see it flourish — though, perhaps, in new and unexpected forms.

1. *Nearly all councils of churches — local, state, and national — are in a process of what some call "revisioning,"* a process during which the churches involved are rethinking the membership, structure, and focus of the council. This is driven, in most cases, by financial considerations, but it would likely need to happen in any case since the ecclesial and social landscape has dramatically altered in recent years.

What this says to me is that this revisioning need not be seen as a sign of illness, but, at least potentially, as an indication of health. A healthy body asks not just "Can the organization survive?" but "What is God doing in this place?" and "How can our churches be part of it?" As leaders in a council rethink its direction and purpose, there is a temptation to start by talking about structure and funding. The place to begin, however, is surely with

1. See Diane Kessler and Michael Kinnamon, *Councils of Churches and the Ecumenical Vision* (Geneva: WCC, 2000); Michael Kinnamon, *The Vision of the Ecumenical Movement and How It Has Been Impoverished by Its Friends* (St. Louis: Chalice Press, 2003), pp. 87-97; and Michael Kinnamon, "Regional and National Councils of Churches," in *The Oxford Handbook of Ecumenical Studies,* forthcoming.

mission: How can a careful look at the mission needs of our location help us discern what God is calling us to be and do together?

The process of revisioning also requires church leaders to distinguish between immediate "problems" and long-term "conditions." Shrinking budgets in a time of financial crisis may be a problem that member churches can, to some extent, "fix" through cuts in expenditures and increases in development activity. Beneath this problem, however, are major shifts, changed conditions that do not lend themselves to quick solutions. The growing religious diversity of this culture, for example, is not a problem to be fixed by changes in mission strategy; it is, in my judgment, a changed condition through which we may learn more about God's one creation.

Similarly, it could be that the problem of decreasing income may force conciliar leaders to ask deeper questions. For example: What new shape should the council take in an era when networking is replacing centralized structures? Even as we must act decisively in response to lean-time problems, can we risk learning new ways of expressing our unity in Christ in the midst of changing conditions? And, Will God grant us the wisdom to know the difference?

2. *There is increasing recognition that the key issue for any council of churches is the commitment and accountability of the churches to one another.* Councils are often regarded as organizations alongside the churches, but this misses the essential point. Councils of churches are not *organizations* that the churches join, so much as *commitments* they make to one another to express something of their unity in Christ and to carry out mission together in his name.[2] This is especially true at the state and national levels, where the defining documents generally speak of the council as a "community" or "fellowship" of the churches. City or regional councils are often seen more as program agencies, as providers of direct services on behalf of the churches; but, even here, the fact of church "ownership" usually makes them unlike other community agencies.

The revisioning process mentioned above provides good chance for conciliar leaders to emphasize relationship building — through such things as church to church visits, increased opportunities for prayer and fellowship, or ample time for sharing joys and concerns in the context of the council — not just program and structure.[3] It also gives councils an opportunity to develop "marks of commitment" (i.e., a public statement of the

2. See Kinnamon, *The Vision of the Ecumenical Movement*, pp. 88-91.
3. See chapter 2 above.

commitments the member churches make to each other) and to underscore the responsibility of the council's staff to hold the churches accountable to those commitments. Church leaders might be invited to sign and period- ically renew the "marks of commitment," with copies available for posting in key church settings.

3. *There is broad agreement that councils of churches at all levels need to relate, in some fashion, to a wider circle of churches* — that their tents are too small. Most councils include only a portion, often a fairly small portion, of the churches in their country, state, or locality. Leaders almost always ex- press a desire to expand the confessional range of churches involved, which usually means reaching out to evangelical and Pentecostal churches, but also to Roman Catholics where they are not already members. There are, however, two challenges to bear in mind. One is the obvious tension be- tween comprehensiveness and prophetic witness — the wider the circle, the more difficult it is to take common stands on pressing issues. The other is the challenge of increasing breadth while, at the same time, maintaining the depth of relationships among longtime members.

With those challenges in mind, some councils are now exploring dif- ferent categories of relationship — members, associate members, partners, friends — while others are considering "hybrid" models in which non- member churches and/or other organizations associate themselves with particular programs or public statements without becoming full members. Such exploration is laudable because it makes room for churches that have not found membership to be compatible with their ecclesiology and sense of mission. The risk is that it will weaken the sense of mutual accountabil- ity, spoken about above, that ought to go with membership in a council of churches.

4. *Councils of churches across the country are discussing how to deal with new divisive issues.* Matters of human sexuality, to take the most obvious example, are splitting the churches both internally and from one another — and, thus, would seem to be obvious topics for ecumenical dialogue. There is reluctance, however, to address these new sources of division within councils. To put it bluntly, many councils of churches are marked by a polite but distant coexistence that avoids contentious issues, which makes it impos- sible for the churches to learn from one another or to seek God's guidance together. I am convinced that a vital council is one in which the churches dare to bring their deepest fears, passions, and conflicts to the table because they affirm their given unity in Christ, even when confronted with genuine disagreement. This point — that Christian unity is more profound than hu-

man agreement[4] and that churches, therefore, should be able to wrestle with difficult matters without weakening their conciliar bonds — is often affirmed in theory but seldom followed in actual practice.

One theologian who has made this case powerfully is Mark Heim. We need, he writes, a new ecumenical movement, one that can

> address our contemporary divisions with the same seriousness and diligence that earlier ecumenical pioneers addressed the traditional theological issues of the fourth and sixteenth centuries. . . . Two generations ago, it was difficult for denominations to speak of each other without heavy doses of ignorance and demonization. Today it is equally hard for differing parties in the Christian culture wars to do so.[5]

Councils of churches, properly understood, are settings in which churches can find challenge and comfort, as well as discover creative energy, through examining tough questions together.

5. *Most councils of churches, including at the state and national level, are looking for ways to involve congregations more directly.* As one state council executive puts it, "Congregations, not denominations, are the new center of our universe" — especially at the state level where middle judicatories are struggling for funding and a clear sense of mission in the changing landscape of denominational life. Congregations often have more vitality than the denominational offices; and many of the most vital congregations are not affiliated, or only loosely affiliated, with any denomination. Councils that are not directly in touch with such congregations are out of touch with sources of energy in the church.

It is important, however, that congregations be seen as full partners in the work of the council, not simply as delivery systems for programs devised by others. Conciliar boards obviously need to include persons who are not bishops or other judicatory leaders; and when taking any action, council leaders need to ask, "What are the implications of this for congregational life?"

6. *A number of councils are expressing a desire to be not only prophetic but pastoral.* Councils of churches, especially national and state, have been engaged not in *lobbying* (which exerts political influence on behalf of those

---

4. For a full treatment of this theme, see Kinnamon, *The Vision of the Ecumenical Movement*, pp. 17-18.

5. S. Mark Heim, "The Next Ecumenical Movement," *Christian Century* (August 14-21, 1996): 782.

with resources) but in *advocacy* (which exerts influence on behalf of those without voice or resources). I want to affirm the importance and appropriateness of such ministry, but also to acknowledge that if this dominates the agenda, then councils deserve the reputation of being "too political."[6] Prayer, not politics, is the heart of the ecumenical movement. Or, to say it another way, the churches' political engagements must flow from their theological base and shared worship of God.

Understood in this way, councils are settings in which churches make praying for one another a priority. The council staff might post prayer concerns named by the member churches, and church leaders would urge their congregations to consult these regularly and to incorporate them into their intercessions. The council would also be a framework for standing with one another in tough times. For example, through a state or local council, churches might be present pastorally with one another when a congregation closes. This is a case of turning difficulty into asset. Since they cannot point contentedly to institutional success, councils have an opportunity to affirm that God is the Chief Actor in this movement — or it does not move at all!

7. *There is lots of discussion in councils of churches about how best to relate to interfaith partners.* The growing religious diversity in the United States surely makes this conversation imperative, though tricky. The desire for closer relations with Jews, Muslims, and other interfaith neighbors may cut against the desire, discussed above, to include more evangelical and Pentecostal churches in the fellowship of the council. Thus, the question is always how to foster structured forms of relationship with other faith communities without losing a central concern for Christian unity and common witness to Jesus Christ.

Of course, in a number of places, councils of churches have restructured to become interfaith. I understand this impulse, especially in local settings where the purpose is to provide direct service, and where there simply aren't enough funds to have both a council of churches and an interfaith organization. I urge conciliar leaders to keep in mind, however, that Christian ecumenism and interfaith relations have different goals, reflecting different theological foundations. The ecumenical vision that gave rise to councils of churches is to express the communion that Christians have with one another through Christ, in order to witness to the gospel and to participate more faithfully and effectively in God's reconciling mission. Thus, to become an interfaith body is not simply a matter of expanding the circle. There may be

6. See chapter 7 above.

good reason to develop an interfaith organization in a particular city, region, or state — but not, if possible, as a substitute for a council of churches.[7]

8. *Conciliar leaders across the country lament that African American churches, and those of other racial or ethnic minorities, are not fully involved.* Such churches may be members of the local or state councils, and there may even be a handful of representatives from minority churches who attend meetings — but most councils remain predominantly white in terms of leadership and ethos.

Part of the reason may be simply a lack of time. Many black pastors lead congregations *and* work at other full-time jobs. For them to be engaged, a council's events and meetings will need to accommodate such schedules. A bigger problem, however, is that churches cannot invite "others" to join an existing reality and expect them to participate fully. A process of revisioning is an opportune moment for racial/ethnic churches to be involved from the ground up. Ask *all* of the churches: What issues are of greatest importance to you? How might the council be organized so that you feel at home in it? Where does your church discern God doing a new thing? What would enhance your sense of oneness with the other members?

9. *Board membership is being debated in nearly every state or local council with which I have had contact.* In some places, judicatory leaders are not on the boards; in others, the board is composed only of these leaders. It is an old argument in ecumenical circles: You need church leaders involved if actions taken by the council's board or assembly are to be implemented, but when they are appointed to the board, these leaders often send surrogates. If bishops and other judicatory leaders do come to the meetings, it is difficult for them, given the crush of other responsibilities, to sustain energy and attention once they leave — assuming they are passionate and knowledgeable about an ecumenical vision of church to begin with!

Beyond these concerns about the participation and commitment of church leaders, there is an obvious need for others in the body of Christ, especially young adults, to play a greater role in conciliar decision making. *Every* council expresses a desire to involve a new generation in the ecumenical movement. Being truly serious about that, however, means making space for younger persons to lead — now. A middle ground, being envisioned in several places, is a board made up of people who are committed and diverse (including chronologically), with a meeting of judicatory leaders held once a year in conjunction with the board.

---

7. See Kinnamon, *The Vision of the Ecumenical Movement*, pp. 105-7.

10. *It follows that there is also widespread reassessment of the programs carried out by councils of churches.* Generally speaking, councils are trying to undertake programs that are carefully selected (out of desire to do a few things well), of limited duration, strongly supported by the members, clearly consistent with the council's overall mission, and for which the council has adequate capacity in terms of persons and finances. One pressing question (noted above) is whether churches should be able to "buy in" to particular programs while opting out of others. This pick-and-choose approach avoids some level of controversy, but it also risks weakening the council as a community or fellowship of churches.

A creative possibility for programming in lean times is for one church or group of churches to give leadership on behalf of the whole council to ministries for which they have special strength and interest. If the Roman Catholic Church in a given region has taken a lead with regard to immigration reform and the protection of immigrants, might its staff person with the immigration portfolio serve, as well, for the whole council? If the Church of the Brethren has a passion for peacemaking ministry, might it represent the entire council when advocacy is needed on behalf of peace? If the United Methodist Church has a particular calling to environmental protection, might it share materials and staff time, when it comes to this issue, with the other members of the council? The council would then be seen as the community within which such sharing of gifts is encouraged and facilitated.[8]

11. *There is a good deal of conversation about the place of Faith and Order in more local ecumenism.* Faith and Order is that stream of the ecumenical movement aimed at overcoming the doctrinal barriers between churches — barriers that hinder the mutual recognition of members and ministers, the shared celebration of the eucharist, the common confession of the apostolic faith, and the ability to make decisions together. *Every* council should surely be concerned about such issues, but I frequently hear objections to having a Faith and Order committee in state or local councils: This is not the level of the church at which decisions about such matters are made. Not all churches have persons locally who can participate creatively in such discussions. It is better to get at theological questions more indirectly, allowing them to arise out of particular situations.

8. A similar approach has been taken in recent years by the National Council of Churches where staff persons in peacemaking and racial justice have been supported financially by the Church of the Brethren and the United Church of Christ, respectively, working for both the council and the denomination.

I have sympathy for these arguments. But I still believe there is a legitimate Faith and Order function in state and local councils. A committee on Faith and Order can

- help "receive" ecumenical agreements (e.g., Baptism, Eucharist and Ministry, and the Joint Declaration on Justification) arrived at through national or international dialogue. The committee can help demonstrate the relevance of such texts for congregational life, and help churches not directly involved in the dialogue see why and how the issues are important for them;
- address divisive matters that may be of particular concern in that place (e.g., the churches' relationship with the Mormon community);
- help the churches engage denominational texts that have implications for the common good (e.g., the 2009 pastoral letter of the United Methodist bishops, "God's Renewed Creation");
- help the churches reflect on the meaning of their life together in the council, perhaps by asking questions about the churches' accountability to one another and whether the churches have grown closer as a result of their conciliar membership;
- keep the concern for visible church unity front and center on the council's agenda.

12. *My experiences around the country repeatedly convince me of the need — the great need! — for a network of local, regional, and state councils of churches, and for colleagues in this work to be in regular contact, sharing best practices and offering mutual support.* For a number of years, the National Council of Churches (NCC) has helped provide such a network through a commission or committee on local and regional ecumenism. Meanwhile, leaders of various ecumenical and interfaith organizations have met annually as the National Association of Ecumenical and Interreligious Staff (NAEIS) — now called the Ecumenical and Interreligious Leaders Network (EILN). It is not clear, however, that the NCC, given its own financial challenges, will be able to continue offering staff support for gatherings of representatives from state and local councils. And, faced with financial constriction, many councils have eliminated funding for staff and elected leaders to attend meetings of the EILN. I obviously regard this as short-sighted. The pressures of guiding councils in lean times, and the peculiar challenges raised by this era, make it more imperative than ever for councils to learn from and support one another.

13. *I hear the following question from different quarters: Is there a role for councils of churches to play when it comes to ecumenical formation?* It seems increasingly clear that new ministers are not learning about the ecumenical movement or being shaped by a vision of Christ's one body in their denominations or denominational seminaries. As a result, ecumenical organizations are still relying far too heavily for leadership on a generation nurtured in the momentum-filled decades following the founding of the World Council of Churches and Vatican II — a very different ecumenical context from the present. Does this mean that councils should see it as major part of their agendas to sponsor workshops and other opportunities to teach a vision of the church united and renewed?

14. *Funding is, of course, a significant concern for nearly every council of churches,* since councils rely, for at least part of their revenue, on churches that are themselves increasingly squeezed. It would seem that, when resources are reduced, churches would begin to do ecumenically what they can no longer afford to do denominationally; but that has not generally proved to be the case. Some local councils are moving to fee-for-service programs in order to generate income, but that makes it all the more difficult to maintain a conciliar identity (i.e., of the churches expressing their essential oneness in Christ together). Most colleagues with whom I speak are urging their boards not simply to whittle away at the present staff and structure (which, in many cases, is no longer possible), but to rethink in a more radical way what it will take to make the council sustainable — even if that means the death of the present organizational structure.

Most churches profess in their official documents that ecumenism is vital to their communion's identity, but the question is what they actually do in lean times. Is ecumenical dialogue and witness something a church supports out of its excess, but cuts when resources shrink (an expendable add-on to the "real" work of the church), or does it see life with others as central to its own self-understanding and spiritual well-being? Times like these *could* be an opportunity to take seriously the famous (and famously ignored) Lund Principle: Churches should "act together in all matters except those in which deep differences of conviction compel [them] to act separately."[9] Or times like these can reinforce the pull toward ecclesiastical introversion, which is always the greatest obstacle to manifesting unity.

I put the matter of funding last not because finances are of little importance, but because, in my judgment, finances are usually a manifestation of

9. See chapter 8.

deeper concerns. As I note at greater length in chapter 14, there is always a temptation, when faced with structural or financial challenges, to make "orthopedic" changes when the real problems are "cardiac." That is to say, real change in councils requires deep-seated change in the churches that constitute them. This is the greatest challenge for councils of churches in this, or any, era.

CHAPTER 13

What Does It Take to Be an Ecumenical Leader?

I have asked this question of colleagues in ecumenical positions numerous times over the years. Generally they name such things as

- an ability to bear indifference with equanimity;
- a willingness to suffer the question, "When did you leave ministry?";
- a capacity to survive on little income;
- skin the thickness of an armadillo's;
- a high threshold for bishop types; and
- a posterior that can withstand endless church meetings.

Such a list has much to commend it! There are, however, other qualities we would do well to identify and confirm — and that is the purpose of this chapter.

At first glance, there would seem to be a small audience for what follows: namely, those few persons called to professional leadership in a council of churches or similar ecumenical organization. Thinking about the qualities needed for ecumenical leadership can also be of value, however, to bishops and other judicatory leaders, congregational ministers, and laypersons who are charged with selecting, evaluating, and supporting professional ecumenists. It may be of help in identifying a new generation of potential leaders. And beyond that, I hope that these reflections are of interest to any leaders in congregations and denominational structures who want their ministry to be marked by ecumenical sensitivity. (An "afterword" on the essential qualities of an ecumenically sensitive bishop addresses the latter point directly.)

Not much has been written on this subject.[1] Job descriptions for council directors often draw on models borrowed from (1) corporate management — understanding of budgets, experience with fundraising, ability to deal with personnel issues — and (2) general ministerial practice — deep faith commitment, love of people (with all their warts), knowledge of the church, sense of compassion, and willingness to encourage lay leadership (even when maddeningly inefficient). Such traits and skills are of real importance, but they don't yet name the distinctive qualities and capacities needed for *ecumenical* leadership. How should the ecumenical mandate of promoting a visibly united church, and the distinctive nature and purpose of an ecumenical council, shape our expectations for leadership? When we speak of ecumenical sensitivity, what should we have in mind?

Essential Qualities

I have been both a volunteer and professional leader in councils of churches and other interchurch organizations since 1980, but the following list of twelve qualities does not presume that my own experience is a model to be emulated. Rather, it is an attempt to distill lessons, both good and bad, that I have learned from observing others during more than three decades of work in the ecumenical movement.

1. *A compelling, even infectious, vision of God's intended wholeness for church and world.*

It is not the task of an ecumenical leader to unite the churches or bring about justice in the human community. It *is* that leader's task to remind the churches that "just as the body is one and has many members, and all the members of the body, though many, are one body, so it is with Christ" (1 Cor. 12:12), and to help them envision the day when "nation shall not lift up sword against nation, neither shall they learn war any more" (Isa. 2:4). A leader isn't expected to concoct a new vision for the churches or ecumenical organizations, but she or he *is* expected to lift up the scripturally rooted vision of what God has done, is doing, and will do to reconcile those who are estranged. This point is memorably stated in the "Message" from the World Council of Churches' (WCC) first assembly (Amsterdam, 1948):

1. See Diane Kessler and Michael Kinnamon, *Councils of Churches and the Ecumenical Vision* (Geneva: WCC, 2000), pp. 53-62. These pages were primarily written by Diane Kessler, which is why I refer to her work on the topic at several points in this chapter.

It is not in man's power to banish sin and death from the earth, to create the unity of the Holy Catholic Church, to conquer the hosts of Satan. But it is within the power of God. He has given us at Easter the certainty that His purpose will be accomplished. But, by our acts of obedience and faith, we can on earth set up signs which point to the coming victory.[2]

The first responsibility of an ecumenical leader is to call the churches to "set up signs" and otherwise participate in God's reconciling mission — even when, especially when, the churches don't want to hear or heed that calling.

Vision, of course, is an essential quality for those in any endeavor who aspire to be leaders rather than managers. Vision is what enables leaders not to overlook but to look beyond short-term problems. And I stress the adjectives *compelling* and *infectious* because ecumenical leaders must communicate this vision through their words, actions, and demeanor in a way that inspires others to long-term commitment.

2. *A capacity for empathy that enables leaders to see from inside a tradition not their own.*

It is important to know *about* other church traditions; but, of course, it is possible to have read about them without having the kind of empathetic identification I have in mind. This involves careful listening and observing as churches define themselves — their heroes and treasured practices, their defining doctrines and historical events, their deepest fears and hopes. And the test of such empathy is when others recognize themselves in what you say about them. My most gratifying moments in ecumenical ministry come when church leaders say to me, "You know us as well as we know ourselves."

There is, however, a difficult side to such empathy. To give one example, even if an ecumenical leader is convinced (as I am) that women are proper candidates for ordained ministry, he or she must still be able to understand — really understand — why some churches, in good faith, disagree. Later in this list of leadership qualities (number 10), I will emphasize that ecumenical leaders are not simply neutral arbiters who must hide their own convictions. *But* all parties in the conciliar community should know that in the person of the leader their integrity is respected and their position understood.

I want only to add that ecumenical leaders, like all Christian ministers, need to have their roots firmly planted in the soil of a particular church. This

2. "'Message' of the first assembly of the WCC," in Michael Kinnamon and Brian E. Cope, eds., *The Ecumenical Movement: An Anthology of Key Texts and Voices* (Grand Rapids: Eerdmans, 1997), p. 22.

identification with one's own church, however, should allow her or him to appreciate the strong identification others have with theirs — and understand why they find it attractive.

3. *A willingness to tolerate anxiety when faced with the unfamiliar.*

An ecumenical leader needs to feel at home — or, at least, as much at home as possible — with an African American altar call, an Orthodox service filled with Greek, and a Moravian Love Feast — perhaps even on the same day! I have heard colleagues in local ecumenical work describe themselves as "professional denominational party crashers" who show up at other people's sacred events as a sign of the wider church. And that's not always easy. Diane Kessler, drawing on her years of experience with the Massachusetts Council of Churches, names an experience known to every ecumenical leader:

> Not many people can walk into a room of difference and feel comfortable immediately. Whether you are the lone woman entering a room filled with male clerics, or a Protestant pastor attending an Orthodox dinner with robed and bearded priests, or a black professional in a dominantly white environment, you may feel an initial pang in the pit of your stomach.[3]

The best solution when feeling such anxiety — when uncertain, for example, about matters of protocol — is, quite simply, to ask questions. At worst, this may communicate a naiveté; but more likely it will communicate a desire to understand from the inside what it feels like to be part of another tradition. And it will help increase one's level of comfort until the foreign becomes familiar.

To put it theologically, an ecumenical leader should demonstrate an appreciation for the catholicity of the church, which encompasses such a wondrous variety of cultures and histories, and for the diversity of gifts that God has given churches to hold in trust for the whole body. Such appreciation will inevitably mean learning on the job — and all the anxiety that goes with it.

4. *An appreciation for the ecumenical movement and for the integration of its often-seemingly-divergent streams.*

It is obviously important for an ecumenical leader to know something of the history and major themes of the ecumenical movement, to see his or her own organization in the context of this global effort to be the church God wills. (For those who need a good introduction, I have an anthology

---

3. Kessler and Kinnamon, *Councils of Churches,* p. 55.

to recommend.[4]) What I really want to emphasize, however, is a crucial appreciation (to use a familiar image) for the multiple streams that feed the ecumenical river. Ecumenism is not just shared advocacy on behalf of peace and justice or dialogues aimed at resolving theological differences or common prayer for the unity of the church or work and dialogue with neighbors of other faiths or common curriculum development and Bible translation or shared service to those in need or witness together in the name of Christ. It is all of these things and more, not as parallel initiatives but as integrated dimensions of a single movement that deals with "the whole task of the whole Church to bring the Gospel to the whole world."[5]

In developing this list of leadership qualities, I might well have said that an ecumenical leader must have a passion for justice — which is true. Or I might have said than an ecumenical leader must have an unshakable commitment to the unity of the church — which is also true. Even more, however, a leader in this movement must be able to hold unity and justice in tension, and to insist that others do the same, even when that tension seems nearly unbearable.[6] Other members of a council staff may have particular portfolios for which they are responsible, and church representatives may be associated with particular programs or parts of the agenda that they champion. But the leader must see the bigger picture and help others see their own work as part of an interdependent whole.

5. *The humility to put themselves, and the structure of the organizations they lead, in the background.*

Elsewhere in this book I develop the idea that the essence of a council of churches is the relationship of the member churches to one another, not their relationship to the structure of the council.[7] In my own ministry at the National Council of Churches (NCC), I tried to insist that, when people think of the council, they should think first of a community of thirty-seven churches, not of an office and a staff in New York and Washington, D.C. This may be less true of other interchurch organizations; but, whatever the ecumenical setting, the biblical mandate for the movement is, with the help of God, to build up *the church* in love. An ecumenical leader knows that the success of a council of churches or other ecumenical body is always in service to this larger goal.

4. Kinnamon and Cope, eds., *The Ecumenical Movement.* A revised edition of this anthology, with Antonios Kireopoulos as co-editor, is forthcoming from the WCC .

5. This quotation is from a meeting of the WCC's Central Committee in 1951. Quoted in Kinnamon and Cope, eds., *The Ecumenical Movement*, p. 5.

6. See chapter 6.

7. See chapters 2 and 12.

This insight has obvious implications for the exercise of leadership. It will often be easier — far easier — for the professional ecumenist to offer public witness on behalf of the churches than to facilitate their doing so; and there are times when this is necessary and appropriate. There are also times, however, when it is necessary and appropriate to take a backseat, even when the leader has done all the preliminary work, in order that the church-centered character of all ecumenical endeavor shines through. Leaders need to lead, but that often means having the humility not to be out front.

6. *The courage to hold the churches accountable to the commitments they make to one another.*

This point and the previous one, while having implications for ecumenical leadership in general, are particularly applicable to those involved with councils of churches (i.e., fellowships in which churches commit themselves, to some extent, to one another). The previous point shows one side of the coin: A council *is* the relationship of the churches. It is not the task of the staff, even the staff leader, to make decisions for the churches. But, on the other side of the coin, it *is* the job of the staff, especially the staff leader, to hold the churches accountable to the commitments they have made with and to one another by virtue of membership in the council.

When I became general secretary of the NCC, I was told by nervous church executives that the council could have nothing to say about the explosive issue of homosexuality, because the churches had no common position on it. That, however, is not true. The NCC's 1995 policy statement on human rights explicitly acknowledges that sexual orientation has been used as a basis for discrimination in housing and employment, and it laments that persons who are lesbian, gay, and bisexual are often the objects of violence and oppression. "The church," in the words of the policy statement, "must stand with those persons whose human rights are abridged or denied on the basis of sexual orientation."[8] It was, therefore, my responsibility to prod the churches to live up to this policy. The churches have *not* spoken a common word on same-sex marriage; thus, it was also my responsibility to hold open *that* dialogue, but always within the framework of what the churches have already said about discrimination.

Holding others accountable to their own commitments will not make one very popular. Having the courage to do so, however, is a key mark of ecumenical leadership.

---

8. "Human Rights: The Fulfillment of Life in the Social Order," at http://www.ncccusa .org/NCCpolicies/humanrights.fulfillmentoflife.htm.

7. An ability to live with disagreement, even conflict, and to encourage others to use it constructively.

Part of the role of an ecumenical leader is to promote dialogue, to create an environment in which the churches bend toward one another. The real test of leadership, however, comes when churches disagree, even to the point of verbal conflict.

In my judgment, the foundation for using conflict constructively is the biblically grounded conviction, often repeated in ecumenical documents, that the unity of the body of Christ is God's gift, not a human achievement. Christian unity, in the words of an early Faith and Order conference, "does not consist in the agreement of our minds or the consent of our wills. . . . We are one because we are all the objects of the love and grace of God."[9] Of course, there *are* theological (and other) differences that need to be reconciled if churches are to confess Jesus Christ together before the world. But the hard work of reaching agreement through dialogue is a consequence of our fundamental communion in Christ, not a prerequisite for it. If this insight were taken to heart, then churches should be able to disagree passionately while staying at the table. An ecumenical leader will want to make this point *before* conflict comes in order that, when it does, it won't be an excuse to divide the body.

Actually, in my experience, churches in conciliar settings often *avoid* disagreement for fear of division, settling for a polite coexistence that sweeps theologically contentious matters under the rug. Councils of churches and similar ecumenical organizations should be places where churches dare to bring their deepest fears and passions, their hardest questions about one another. An ecumenical leader will encourage this level of sharing, will insist that a willingness to deal with difficult issues in love is itself a most powerful witness to God's reconciling grace.

Various councils in the U.S. have developed helpful guidelines, not just for conflict resolution, but for using conflict constructively. The National Council of Churches in Australia has also produced materials that can be of help to ecumenical leaders and the bodies they serve.[10]

8. An appreciation that the church is both local and universal, and a willingness to hold them together.

Ecumenical leaders should have what we might call a "love for the local"

---

9. "Affirmation of Union in Allegiance to Our Lord Jesus Christ," in Kinnamon and Cope, eds., *The Ecumenical Movement*, p. 85.

10. "Australian Churches Covenanting Together," at http://ecumenism.net/archive/docu/2004_australian_covenant.pdf.

— a desire to see the ecumenical vision take root in congregations, parishes, and dioceses — coupled with an "appreciation for the global." This quality of leadership reflects the crucial ecclesiological principle that the church is *both* the local gathering of believers in which Christ dwells by faith *and* the universal body through which believers of differing nations and cultures are bound to one another. The local is not merely a branch office of the universal, and the universal is not merely an aggregate of the local. The word *church* is properly used for both because they are fully interdependent.[11]

In the same way, there is one ecumenical movement through which the unity and renewal of the whole church, local and universal, is promoted. Leaders of local ecumenical organizations should be aware of the issues facing — and make use of materials produced by — the WCC and the international dialogues, even as colleagues in those settings should be fully attentive to the distinctive challenges of local ecumenism.

9. A recognition that the authority of an ecumenical leader is (only) "charismatic," coupled with a capacity to exercise it.

The authority of a council of churches, to borrow a phrase used by William Temple with regard to the WCC, consists only "in the weight which it carries with the churches by its own wisdom."[12] In other words, the governing body of a council or other ecumenical organization cannot command the obedience of the churches or speak in any name but its own.

This has obvious implications for the authority of professional ecumenical leaders. The NCC's (former) Commission on Regional and Local Ecumenism, in a set of "Guidelines for Ecumenical Leadership," argued that "there is virtually no authority vested in the ecumenical leader"; he or she must, therefore, "be able to build partnerships with diverse people and communities in order to model the shared leadership required for the ecumenical task."[13] But, while the last part of this statement is helpful, the first part goes too far. There is virtually no authority vested in the *office* of an ecumenical leader, but surely those charged with responsibility for ecumenical bodies must have what Max Weber called "charismatic authority" — authority which rests on the wisdom and exemplary character of the leader, authority grounded in personal qualities that inspire confidence and respect.

---

11. See chapter 4.

12. William Temple, "Explanatory Memorandum on the Constitution of the World Council of Churches," in W. A. Visser 't Hooft, *The Genesis and Formation of the World Council of Churches* (Geneva: WCC, 1982), p. 109.

13. "Guidelines for Ecumenical Leadership," at http://www.naeis.org/pdf/Leadership Guidelines.pdf.

In theory, when churches choose someone to fill the position of ecumenical leader, they are saying that they want him or her to function in ways that exhibit charismatic authority. In practice, however, the authority of an ecumenical leader is always precarious. It is essential to teach and act in a way that encourages others to follow, without claiming more authority than is warranted by the nature of an ecumenical organization. It is a fine line to walk!

At the NCC, I insisted on making general secretary's reports to the Governing Board and General Assembly that were quite extensive in order to assert my role as one who named issues for common consideration and set the work of the council in wider perspective. The reports were also heavy on references to the church's theological traditions and to our shared ecumenical heritage in order to ground them in commonly claimed sources of authority. This, however, is only a single strategy within what must be a whole mode of exercising leadership. Theological acumen gave me authority in certain parts of the council's agenda and constituency; a more tentative grasp of finances undoubtedly undermined it in others.

10. *A strong conviction that this work is ministry, and that it includes a responsibility to teach the gospel.*

In our book on councils of churches, Diane Kessler and I stress that "first and foremost, ecumenical administration is a form of ministry rooted in our baptism."[14] Such an orientation should remind ecumenical leaders (a) that they are connected to the people with whom they work by far more than shared interests, and (b) that they have an ongoing responsibility to proclaim and teach the gospel as they understand it.

This is a subtle point, but one of great importance. An ecumenical leader is not simply a monitor of the churches' conversation. In selecting her or him for a position of ecumenical *ministry,* the churches are expressing their trust in that person's capacity to interpret the gospel with integrity and insight. This does not mean that others will always affirm the leader's interpretations. But it does mean that those involved with the organization must take what the leader says seriously, and that they should treat the ecumenical leader as minister, not simply as administrator.

11. *The spiritual depth to sustain one in the face of inevitable loneliness and frustration.*

Let's say it boldly: Churches do not generally rush to embrace an ecumenical identity! They may cooperate, to the extent dwindling resources allow, but ecumenism is usually tacked on to what they regard as their

14. Kessler and Kinnamon, *Councils of Churches,* p. 53.

"real work and identity." Thus, the tenacity demanded to keep declaring the churches' need for one another takes spiritual depth, rooted, I believe, in the disciplines of regular prayer and study of Scripture. An ecumenical leader without a mature spiritual life will soon lose energy for the task.

Beyond that, ecumenical ministry can be quite isolating. As Diane Kessler puts it, "Few people will tell you to take care of yourself. Few, if any, will notice if you spend all those extra hours working. Few will tell you that you've done a good job."[15] To avoid burnout, an ecumenical leader needs to stay grounded in a congregation, maintain strong connections with his or her denomination, and find or create a community of colleagues who provide counsel and support. I also recommend taking full advantage of wider opportunities for collegial contact, such as those provided by the electronic newsletter and meetings of the Ecumenical and Interreligious Leaders Network.

12. *An unshakable hope in God's future.*

I am not talking about being optimistic;[16] there may be many "ecumenical winters" in the coming years. I am talking, rather, about the confident expectation that, despite human faithlessness, God will be faithful to the scriptural promises of peace with justice and unity with diversity. An ecumenical leader will help others to see that, whatever the setbacks and frustrations, ecumenical effort is never in vain.

It is often said that ecumenical ministry requires the *patience* of a saint — and that is hard to deny. The unity God has promised will come according to God's timetable, not ours. I am convinced, however, that ecumenical leadership is also marked by a holy *impatience* that, precisely because of our vision of God's future, dares to pray, "Come, Lord Jesus! Heal the divisions of your church, and lead us *now* in the ways of peace."

Afterword: The Ecumenical Bishop

Over the years, I have often been asked what would mark a bishop or other judicatory leader as "ecumenical." What, in other words, would it mean for a diocesan bishop or a regional or conference minister to exercise her or his ministry of oversight in an ecumenically sensitive way? With some fear and trembling, let me offer the following six suggestions:

15. Kessler and Kinnamon, *Councils of Churches*, p. 60.
16. See chapter 14.

1. *Show that ecumenical relationships are a priority by the way you relate to judicatory leaders in other churches.* Pray for each other (sharing prayer concerns online?). Check in regularly with each other (establishing a time for bi-weekly conference calls?). Attend one another's major events and invite others to yours. Modeling ecumenical commitment is, of course, the best way to encourage it in those entrusted to your care.

2. *Encourage congregations/parishes to claim an ecumenical identity by publicly recognizing, even celebrating, their inter-church (and interfaith) activities at your conference or diocesan assemblies.* Since congregations may need help in imagining ecumenical possibilities, you may want to develop a brochure or other resource for this purpose and to distribute a calendar of ecumenical events (e.g., the Week of Prayer for Christian Unity).[17]

3. *Make ecumenical and interfaith leadership a criterion for evaluating ministerial performance.* I know from my own denomination that congregations and ministers are primarily recognized, at least in public settings, for increases in membership and mission giving. That is surely important, but so is engagement with another church or religious community, especially in this era of growing diversity.

4. *Talk about ecumenical and interfaith developments in your reports, newsletters, and other forms of communication with the diocese/region.* Share information about successful models of ecumenical life; point to resources that local folks may find valuable. And, of course, it is always good to lift up themes of reconciliation and peace in your preaching.

5. *Encourage the study and reception of ecumenical initiatives undertaken by your denomination.* Urge congregations to study proposals for new church-to-church relationships as they are being developed, and to implement them as fully as possible once they are inaugurated. A conference/ diocese commission may be needed to help promote such study and implementation — as long as the study is not confined to the commission alone![18]

6. *Regard local and state councils of churches as expressions of your own church's life and ministry.* Councils, as I have argued in other chapters, are not simply service organizations that do things for the churches; they are communities or fellowships constituted by relationships among the churches themselves. This means that conciliar leaders should be invited to report, like any other part of the church, at assemblies and other appropriate venues.[19]

17. Lists of possible ecumenical activities for congregations can be found in chapter 8.
18. One such initiative, full communion relationships, is discussed in chapter 2.
19. Councils of churches are discussed in chapters 2 and 12.

CHAPTER 14

What Will It Take to Revitalize the Ecumenical Movement?

The title of the chapter gives it away: I believe that the ecumenical movement is in great need of revitalization. Walter Kasper, former head of the Vatican's Council for Promoting Christian Unity, puts it more sharply: "After the first wave of enthusiasm, there is now much disenchantment at unfulfilled expectations. We still cannot gather together at the table of the Lord. Ecumenical progress has slowed, with churches often seeming to withdraw into old self-sufficient confessionalism. . . . Ecumenism seems to be in crisis."[1]

I suspect that most, if not all, readers will agree with this assessment. It is by no means the whole story, as I have tried to show in other chapters of this book; but there can be little doubt that the ecumenical movement today lacks the vitality it once had. So instead of arguing that case further, this chapter will explore the contours of the crisis and point in the direction of what it will take for the ecumenical spirit in the churches to be revitalized. Efforts like this are inevitably heavier on diagnosis than on remedy, but diagnosis is not an insignificant task. I will begin by naming four manifestations of weakness in the movement, as I experience it:

1. *Loss of commitment among church leaders to the goal of Christian unity.*
In a 2011 speech at Catholic University of America, Cardinal Kasper's successor in the Vatican office, Kurt Koch, asked pointedly whether Christians "still feel the painful offense of the division of the one body of Christ, or whether we have not in fact adapted to it or even come to terms with it. . . .

---

1. Walter Kasper, "May They All Be One? But How? A Vision of Christian Unity for the Next Generation," *Ecumenical Trends* 40 (April 2011): 4.

What pains me most in the current ecumenical situation," he said, "is the fact that so many Christians today are no longer pained by this profoundly abnormal situation. . . . For where the division of the one body of Christ is no longer perceived as an offense and no longer causes pain, there ecumenism ultimately becomes superfluous."[2]

In my experience, the great ecumenical vision/goal of eucharistic fellowship is reduced, in the minds of many church leaders, to policies of good neighborliness that can easily be demoted on the list of ecclesiastical priorities. There is a widespread willingness to settle for occasional cooperation rather than to press, through dialogues and conciliar relationships, for ever-deeper expressions of unity. Even full communion agreements, which I certainly applaud, seem to be implemented minimally rather than maximally, leading to what I once heard Albert Outler scornfully call "ecumenism within the status quo."

What has brought us to this state of affairs? Well, Kasper is surely correct that disappointment over the lack of concrete results has soured many would-be ecumenists. I have repeatedly watched seminary students get excited by the products of ecumenical dialogue — and, as we have seen, there are many to get excited about — only to grow cynical when they grasp the profound lack of reception in our churches. When expectation outstrips actual accomplishment, energy for the entire effort will be lost.

Of course, my cynical students are not seeing the whole picture. The movement has helped effect a real, if limited, improvement in relations among churches. But, somewhat ironically, this very success has lessened the urgency for further ecumenical advance. We may not be able to share the eucharist or affirm one another's ministries or make much impact on public debates about war or poverty or climate change, but at least we get along! Isn't that enough? Church hopping is now more the rule than the exception. And while this may be more a matter of ecumenism by erosion than mutual enrichment, isn't it the best we can do in this era?

Another factor in the decline of ecumenical passion may be the otherwise laudable improvement in interfaith relations. Many of my students now regard Christian unity as passé, seeing interfaith dialogue as a sexier alternative. They acknowledge that the unity of Christians may have seemed important to our ancestors living in a predominantly Christian society, but the growing religious diversity of our culture has made even eucharistic

2. Kurt Koch, "Fundamental Aspects of Ecumenism and Future Perspectives," an unpublished paper presented November 3, 2011, at Catholic University of America, Washington, D.C.

fellowship seem to them like a narrow, relatively inconsequential aspiration. They may agree with Hans Küng's claim that there will be "no peace among the nations without peace among the religions."[3] But reconciliation among Christians? Will that really make much of a difference?

A more profound reason for decreased ecumenical passion has to do with the postmodern emphasis on particularity. The spirit of this age means that, for many in our culture, unity is at best the tolerant acknowledgement of multiplicity (as if diversity had any real meaning apart from its placement in a greater whole!). In the words of *New York Times* religion columnist Peter Steinfels, "What was once the scandal of division now looks more like the virtue of diversity."[4] A prime example is the United Church of Christ (UCC), which, despite having John 17 ("that all may be one") on its logo, now exalts a multicultural identity on its website, while burying its historic concern for Christian unity in the last paragraph of both its Statement of Mission and Statement of Commitment for the twenty-first century.[5]

Please don't misunderstand me. I celebrate the fact that, in our era, populations that have been excluded from the life or, at least, the decision making of the church now have a prominent place. But I lament the fact that, for whatever reasons, the commitment to unity in Christ has waned among leaders of the UCC and other denominations.

2. *Divisions and other signs of weakness within the ecumenically support-ive churches.*

This could be a subset of the previous point, but I think it warrants more focused attention. The mainline churches — churches that have been the pillars of ecumenical organizations and dialogues — have obviously gone through a period of traumatic transition. Over the past half century, leaders of these denominations have suffered through a steady decline of numbers, resources, and cultural influence; and now they are faced with internal divi-sions over questions of human sexuality. So it is troubling, but not surprising, that mainline Protestants seem content with occasional cooperation, that they are less willing to risk new ecumenical ventures, and that we are wit-nessing a renewed focus on denominational identity. "The looming question for many . . . denominations," writes Steinfels, "is no longer whether doctri-

3. See http://www.scu.edu/ethics/practicing/focusareas/global_ethics/laughlin-lectures/kung-world-religions.html.

4. Peter Steinfels, "Praying for Christian Unity, When Diversity Has Been the Answer," at http://www.nytimes.com/2008/01/19/us/19beliefs.html?_r=0.

5. http://www.ucc.org/beliefs/toward-the-21st-century.html and http://www.ucc.org/beliefs/statement-of-mission.html.

nal boundaries are too absolute and exclusive, but whether these groups can define and maintain any clear-cut identity at all."[6] There is nothing wrong, of course, with wanting to give and receive the distinctive riches of our ecclesial heritages for the sake of building up the one body; but there is a good deal wrong, certainly unscriptural, with emphasizing our church's particularity in order to beat the competition.

I recently spoke to an assembly of one of the conferences of a main-line denomination for which the assembly theme was "Transforming the World by Being United in Christ." There was, however, utterly no mention of promoting unity with other churches in the conference's Vision Statement, Mission Statement, or Statement of Goals and Actions; no reference to doing mission ecumenically overseas in the assembly materials; no reference to ecumenical engagement in its lists of criteria for clergy and congregational excellence; and no report to the assembly from the church's full communion partners or from the state and national councils of churches. The focus was almost entirely on church growth, on burnishing their denominational brand in order to maintain institutional strength. This attitude is reflected in the predatory relationship that so often exists among congregations in this country. Grow or die. Every congregation for itself when it comes to getting new members — as if the eye could contest with the hand to see who gets the foot![7]

My biggest concern, however, is for the loss of theological depth in many churches, which, of course, spills over into their understanding of ecumenism. If our churches no longer believe or can articulate that God has acted in Christ for the world's redemption, then the idea that God has given us a new community in Christ of Jew and Greek, Protestant and Catholic, black and white, gay and straight, Iraqi and American will seem like pure idealism — impossible and ultimately irrelevant. In the absence of such theological conviction, ecumenism will become simply another arena for pursuing political agendas or another set of agencies engaged in cooperation. And who can be passionate about that?

3. *An increasing split between two sets of ecumenical priorities.*

The integration of Faith and Order and Life and Work has never been easy, but today tension has reached the point where it is difficult to speak of one ecumenical movement. As I noted in chapter 6, this division is clearly

6. Steinfels, "Praying for Christian Unity."

7. See Bruce D. Marshall, "Who Really Cares About Christian Unity?" *First Things* 109 (January 2000): 29-34.

visible in the very different constituencies that attend Ecumenical Advocacy Days (EAD) and the National Workshop on Christian Unity. In my experience, most participants at EAD would argue that the fundamental divide in human community is between rich and poor, oppressor and oppressed; and that the basic division in the church has to do with how Christians respond to and participate in these divisions of the world. They use language like "unity in solidarity," and focus not on agreed statements of faith or common structures, but on a shared willingness to act together in response to human need. I have even heard it said at EAD that "splitting theological hairs" with regard to sacraments or ministry or confession of faith is precisely what has turned off many would-be ecumenists.

By contrast, those who attend the National Workshop would generally contend that the church serves the wider human community best when it lives more fully as the church God wills — confessing Christ together, sharing the eucharist, recognizing the baptisms and ordinations performed in other parts of the body, and having a structure that allows, when needed, for common decision making. Addressing these areas of division is, therefore, the highest ecumenical priority and the basis for authentic Christian witness and mission.

Those who have read other chapters in this book likely know my position: that the ecumenical vision is impoverished not by those who start with (even emphasize) either social justice or doctrinal reconciliation, but by those who split the agenda, playing one off against the other.[8] Not all ecumenists agree. For example, the highly respected Lutheran theologian and longtime dialogue participant George Lindbeck has taken explicit exception to my approach, arguing that whenever Faith and Order and Life and Work are regarded as equals, politics ends up dominating theology and the ecumenical movement becomes simply another setting for advancing political goals.[9] This is, indeed, a danger. But in my judgment, the failure to attempt their integration is a bigger one — and a real sign of weakness in the movement.

4. *Diminishment of key instruments of the ecumenical movement, including councils of churches.*

Most councils of churches these days struggle to obtain adequate fund-

---

8. See chapter 6. This theme is developed at greater length in Michael Kinnamon, *The Vision of the Ecumenical Movement and How It Has Been Impoverished by Its Friends* (St. Louis: Chalice Press, 2003), pp. 37-49.

9. George Lindbeck, "Ecumenisms in Conflict," in L. Gregory Jones et al., eds., *God, Truth, and Witness* (Grand Rapids: Brazos Press, 2005), pp. 224-28.

ing for the programs and services authorized by church representatives, with a result that concern for survival takes precedence over innovative thinking. Financial difficulties often lead to restructuring, which frequently means that a reduced staff is asked to do the same amount of work as before. Most national and local councils now include only a portion, often a fairly small portion, of the churches in their country or locality. At the same time, many settings are witnessing a proliferation of inter-church organizations. National councils of churches that have an historic relationship to the wider ecumenical movement now appear, in many countries, to be one among several competing multi-confessional agencies.

The overriding problem councils face, however, is the failure of churches to grasp that the essence of any council of churches is the relationship of the member churches to one another, not their relationship to some structure or office. A council is not so much an organization that churches join as it is a mutual commitment they make in order to form a fellowship or community of churches. Whenever churches regard a conciliar body as "that organization" rather than as "our fellowship," then conciliar life has been radically misunderstood — and the accountability that ought to go with conciliar membership is minimized. Actually, the situation is even more troubling. When councils lose their theological vision, they are in real danger of becoming service organizations aimed at self-perpetuation. And to the extent that happens, their very success can institutionalize present divisions short of the unity for which Christ prayed.[10]

Seeking Remedy

It is tempting, as we move from diagnosis to remedy, to talk specifically about such things as the reorganization of the National Council of Churches. It is tempting, in other words, when confronted with structural or financial challenges, to make "orthopedic" changes when the real problems are "cardiac." With that in mind, I want to name two cardiac-type responses to the weaknesses I have identified:

1. *Renewed emphasis on spiritual ecumenism.*

I say this with some trepidation in light of a recent experience. While teaching an adult church school class in a local congregation, I mentioned

10. See chapters 2 and 12. This idea is developed at greater length in Kinnamon, *The Vision of the Ecumenical Movement*, pp. 87-97.

the Week of Prayer for Christian Unity — which most had never heard of, let alone participated in — and commended it for the following January. At which point one woman practically sneered, "Pray for it! That's what people always say when they can't figure out what to do."

Maybe so. But the ecumenical movement, in my experience, has become so preoccupied with *doing* — conferences, committees, dialogues, reports — that it feels like business as usual rather than something Spirit-led. That's why I have long felt that the movement's single most valuable resource is the ecumenical prayer cycle, *In God's Hands,* which invites the churches to mutual intercession and provides materials to help them engage in this spiritual discipline.[11] Such intercession begins with giving thanks to God for one another, which is already a step beyond old patterns of competition and suspicion. If churches are to pray for one another, they need to know one another far better than is generally the case — each other's needs and hopes, not just their doctrinal positions. Such intercession is never a substitute for practical acts of solidarity. Rather, intercession "is the mobilization of our imaginations on behalf of the others,"[12] signaling a constant readiness to help — and to receive help. Churches, especially western churches, find it easier to give than to receive; but when we intercede for others, we realize that we, too, are in need of intercession. Intercession, in short, leads us to submit our will to God's.

This emphasis on prayer has been articulated by many ecumenical leaders and gatherings. "The measure of our concern for unity," said delegates to the WCC's second assembly in 1954, "is the degree to which we pray for it. We cannot expect God to give us unity unless we prepare ourselves to receive his gift by costly and purifying prayer. To pray together is to be drawn together."[13] The Second Vatican Council's *Decree on Ecumenism* refers to prayer for unity as the "soul of the whole ecumenical movement,"[14] a claim underscored in Pope John Paul II's encyclical *Ut Unum Sint* ("That

11. Hugh McCullum and Terry MacArthur, eds., *In God's Hands: Common Prayer for the World* (Geneva: WCC, 2006).

12. Lukas Vischer, *Intercession* (Geneva: WCC, 1980), 59. I am indebted to Vischer for his clear thinking on this topic. Another fine resource is Walter Kasper, *A Handbook of Spiritual Ecumenism* (Hyde Park, N.Y.: New City Press, 2007).

13. W. A. Visser 't Hooft, ed., *The Evanston Report: The Second Assembly of the World Council of Churches* (London: SCM Press, 1955), p. 91.

14. *Unitatis Redintegratio* (Decree on Ecumenism), par. 8, at http://www.vatican.va/archive/hist_councils/ii_vatican_council/documents/vat-ii_decree_19641121_unitatis-redintegratio_en.html.

They May Be One") and exemplified in such ecumenical communities as Taizé and Iona.

Prayer gives hope in the face of inevitable setback. It reminds us of our fundamental connectedness to others who also call on the name of Christ. Prayer opens us to the reality of God's grace and, thus, invites us to offer our differences in common service. It requires a humbling of ourselves in order to recognize our shared identity as children of God. Since unity is a gift, we ask for it in prayer. But since it is a gift that must be received, our prayer is also for the strength and courage to act upon that which God gives.[15]

Let's say it boldly: God is the Chief Actor in this movement! Whenever ecumenism "moves," it is not *our* achievement we celebrate, but *God's* grace for which we give thanks. The image is a simple one: Since God is the center, the closer we draw to God — or, better, the closer we are drawn to God — the closer we draw to one another. The fact that we can no longer revel in institutional success might just drive us back to this revitalizing realization.

2. *Renewed interest and commitment among the laity.*

It is important to remember that the ecumenical movement began as a lay enterprise — in the mission fields, in the Student Christian Movement, in the World Sunday School Association, in the YMCA and YWCA, in the various Bible societies. It was, in short, a largely lay-driven protest against the stultifying fragmentation of the church. Gradually, however, this protest movement was domesticated, brought under the control of the churches it was intended to reform, and turned into another program or denominational office alongside a host of others (except that the others are usually better funded). Are the Disciples still ecumenical? Why, yes, we have an office in Indianapolis that handles that part of the church's business.[16]

It is possible to overstate the point. Let us give appropriate thanks for bishops who have been ecumenical leaders, and for professional ecumenists. After all, I am one. But if ecumenism is to be revitalized, then it cannot be left for denominational specialists and theological experts to do on behalf of the church. John Cogley, longtime editor of *The Commonweal,* and a lay Catholic, once wrote that just as war is too serious to be left to generals, so Christian unity is too important to be left to priests and bishops.[17] Vatican II came alive, he noted, in the "living room dialogues" of the 1960s.

15. See Emilio Castro, *When We Pray Together* (Geneva: WCC, 1989), p. 1.

16. This is developed at greater length in Kinnamon, *The Vision of the Ecumenical Movement*, pp. 75-86.

17. John Cogley, "Ten Commandments for the Ecumenical Age," in John A. O'Brien, ed., *Steps to Christian Unity* (Garden City, N.Y.: Doubleday, 1964), p. 244.

The Latin American ecumenist and economist Julio de Santa Ana, known for his advocacy on behalf of the poor, ends a recent essay on the future of ecumenism not with a call to social justice, but by arguing that "the challenge of our times is to make ecumenism appealing once again for the educated and activist minded laity."[18]

I want only to add that the younger generations are an especially important part of the laity. I give thanks to God for the generation that came of age during the early decades of the WCC and the years of Vatican II. These people, touched by a vision of common life and mission, have given extraordinary leadership to the ecumenical movement. But if the movement is to have a future, then a new generation of leaders must be grasped by this idea of the church as a sign of wholeness and reconciliation. This will surely mean new priorities and new ways of communicating — if we are open to them.

This chapter is obviously not a detailed prescription for ecumenical revitalization. In my judgment, however, these two priorities should guide efforts at renewal: (1) renewed emphasis on the spiritual foundation of ecumenism; and (2) renewed engagement of the laity, especially younger generations, in the life and leadership of the movement. How these things happen will depend on the creativity of leaders in different contexts. That they should be priorities is, as I see it, beyond question.

Chastened Expectations

It was easier to be an ecumenically minded Christian fifty years ago than it is today! The winds in those days were far more favorable for the ecumenical ship than they have been in the early years of this century. The WCC had come into existence after the Second World War — along with national councils of churches in numerous countries — and despite facing great challenges during its first decade, it was still a sign of hope that a fragmented church might be able to speak with one voice on urgent issues (a parallel to the political hopes inspired by the creation of the U.N.). Between 1947 and 1970, united churches, formed by the union of previously separated denominations, were established in places where European colonialism had meant the exporting of church divisions, including India, the Philippines, Zambia,

18. Julio de Santa Ana, "The Ecumenical Movement at the Crossroads," at http://www .wscfglobal.org/pdfs/247_Art1_SantaAna.pdf.

Jamaica, Papua New Guinea and the Solomon Islands, Ecuador, the Congo, Madagascar, and the United States. And then, in the early 1960s, Vatican II thrust the Roman Catholic Church into the center of ecumenical dialogue, raising hopes that centuries of estrangement — Catholic and Protestant, Catholic and Orthodox — might, at least in part, be overcome.

The late 1960s was also the historical setting for two seminal gatherings sponsored by the WCC: the World Conference on Church and Society, convened in Geneva in 1966, and the council's fourth assembly, which met in Uppsala, Sweden, two years later. The Geneva conference, which came on the heels of Vatican II, was the first major WCC meeting to have a sizable Roman Catholic delegation. It was also the first at which a majority of the participants came from countries outside Europe and North America, a sign of the world-changing independence struggles of that era. It was, of course, a time of tremendous social turmoil in the West as well, so it is not surprising that Geneva '66 was the first ecumenical conference to speak positively of the possibility of revolutionary change. And all of these themes received attention at the assembly in Uppsala. For some, this is when the ecumenical movement began to put itself on the right side of history. For others, this is precisely when it began to go astray.[19]

What strikes me most forcefully, however, is the *optimism* of the reports from these two events, an optimism that stands in stark contrast to the mood of our own era and may serve as a measure of change over the past fifty years. A few quick examples make the point:[20]

- The participants in Geneva a half century ago clearly assumed that economic development was a tide that would lift all boats in the harbor — that economic growth, instead of resulting in the obscene disparity in wealth so evident today, would truly benefit the poor. There was talk of revolution against political systems that inhibit such growth, but little sense of how entrenched economic interests actually are.
- The report from Geneva '66 shows great faith that technological progress would contribute to human betterment. This confidence was still evident at the assembly two years later in Uppsala, which spoke, for example, of "new advances in agriculture [that] hold the promise of

19. See, e.g., Geoffrey Wainwright, "Ecumenism in Transition: A Paradigm Shift in the Ecumenical Movement?" *Midstream* 31 (April 1992): 170.

20. The paragraphs that follow draw heavily from Lukas Vischer, "Committed to the Transformation of the World?" *Ecumenical Review* 59 (January 2007): 27-47.

freedom from hunger."[21] Both meetings show little awareness of the ambiguity of technological achievement, and no awareness of what the Club of Rome, just five years after Uppsala, would call the "limits of growth." Nature was still regarded as a stage for the drama of human redemption, not as the threatened ecosystem we now know it to be.[22]

- Violence was seen as an option, albeit of last resort, that could be used in a limited way to promote social transformation. There was apparently little recognition, so clear to many in the present generation, that violence is inevitably co-opted, that it has a dynamic of its own and is seldom, if ever, limited to its intended purpose.

- There was great optimism at Uppsala, and throughout that decade, in the possibility of real advance toward the visible unity of the church. Church to church dialogues and locally united churches were springing up around the world and in unexpected places.[23] The 1968 assembly was the first to have official Roman Catholic participation, and one Catholic speaker raised the possibility of his church joining the WCC. "The church," in the words of the assembly report, "is bold in speaking of itself as the sign of the coming unity of [hu]mankind"[24] — a statement so aggressively optimistic that it sounds pretentious to our ears. Today we have a library full of theological agreements dealing with Reformation-era disputes, even as we watch churches continue to compete to win new members and to fragment over new issues. Just as Geneva and Uppsala had little sense of how entrenched economic interests are, so they did not predict how entrenched ecclesial interests would continue to be.

I do not mean to suggest that ecumenism has simply gone downhill since 1968! There have been numerous developments that all of us, I trust, regard as positive. At neither Geneva nor Uppsala did women have major leadership roles. Interfaith relations and environmental protection hardly figured in either agenda. Major ecumenical agreements on issues from sacraments to nuclear weapons, from the doctrine of justification to religious pluralism, were still to come. As previous chapters in this book make clear,

21. Norman Goodall, ed., *The Uppsala Report: Official Report of the Fourth Assembly of the World Council of Churches* (Geneva: WCC, 1968), p. 50.

22. See chapter 5.

23. In this country, it was in the late 1960s that work was completed on a (never consummated) Plan of Union involving nine Protestant denominations, known as the Consultation on Church Union.

24. Goodall, ed., *The Uppsala Report*, p. 17.

the churches have begun to say much together about the nature and purpose of the church.

But the point I am trying to make has to do with a marked change in tone. "We know," says the Geneva report, "that God appears to have set no limits to what may be achieved by our generation, if we understand our own problems right and desire to obey in our circumstances."[25] Such statements, writes Lukas Vischer in his insightful analysis of the Geneva conference, "sound today like voices from far away. The confidence that characterized the gathering has vanished. The question today is, rather, to what extent the churches, in the face of political, economic, and ecological [and eccelesial!] complexity, are still capable of any common witness."[26] In my chapter for the third volume of the *History of the Ecumenical Movement*, published in 2004, I call this change "chastened expectations."[27] If ever we could take being ecumenical for granted, we cannot do so now.

And so we return to the question: How can the ecumenical movement be revitalized in such an era? I believe that an answer to this question is suggested in the distinction between optimism and hope. Optimism involves the expectation of a better future based on a reading of present circumstances; hope involves the trustful anticipation of genuine newness, perhaps beyond our imagining, based on the promises of God. The "Message" to the churches from the Geneva conference declares that "as Christians we are committed to working for the transformation of the world."[28] Compare this to the theme from the WCC's 2006 assembly in Porto Alegre, Brazil: "God, in your grace, transform the world." Those who are optimistic speak of what *they* can accomplish. Those who live in hope give thanks for what *God* can and will accomplish, regardless of how difficult the present may seem. Yes, we are called to participate in God's mission, but our activity is understood as a response to the One in whom we hope.

Could it be that a time of chastened expectations leads us to trust more in God's guidance, discerned through shared Bible study and prayer, than in our skill at managing organizations or our capacity for drafting texts? Vatican II's *Decree on Ecumenism* — which, of course, was written in the 1960s — speaks of "change of heart and holiness of life," of prayer "for the

25. Quoted in Vischer, "Committed to the Transformation of the World?" pp. 45-46.

26. Vischer, "Committed to the Transformation of the World?" p. 39.

27. Michael Kinnamon, "Assessing the Ecumenical Movement," in John Briggs et al., eds., *A History of the Ecumenical Movement*, vol. 3 (Geneva: WCC, 2004), p. 54.

28. M. M. Thomas and Paul Albrecht, eds., *World Conference on Church and Society: Official Report* (Geneva: WCC, 1967), p. 48.

grace to be genuinely self-denying, humble, gentle in the service of others"[29] as the essence of the ecumenical movement. Could it be that, in the absence of reasons to be optimistic, we discover greater humility and gentleness in our relations with sisters and brothers in other churches? Could it be that less optimism and more hope allows us to let go of favored projects and structures, while holding fast to those promises of God's reign that commonly compel us? Isn't this a key to the movement's revitalization?

Ecumenical Christians today may be less optimistic than our earlier colleagues, but surely we have no less reason to hope for the day when one part of Christ's body will not say of another, "We have no need of you." Perhaps our role in such a time as this is to keep alive such hope — and to call ourselves to demonstrate the credibility of our hope by acting together, in response to God, to help make it so.

29. *Decree on Ecumenism,* par. 7.

CHAPTER 15

Why Care About Christian Unity When There Are So Many Other Things to Worry About?

We all know what an oxymoron is: words used together that don't really seem to belong with one another — like jumbo shrimp or Quaker hit man or House Intelligence Committee (or united Methodists?). How about fighting Amish? Somehow it doesn't seem right, downright oxymoronic, to read about Amish invading the homes of other Amish in order to cut off the men's beards and the women's hair; but that, of course, is what happened in 2010 in an Amish community south of Cleveland, Ohio. What I want to suggest in this brief final chapter is that, if Scripture is our guide, the very idea of a "divided church" is just as much an oxymoron.

The New Testament spells this out with remarkable clarity. Whatever else the church may be, it is the body of Christ — and Christ cannot be divided. Remember the language used in Ephesians: "*Maintain* the unity of the Spirit in the bond of peace. There *is* one body . . . one Lord, one faith, one baptism, one God and Father of all, who is above all and through all and in all" (4:3-6). Paul doesn't say that the eye and the hand ought to negotiate in order to form a body. No! We *are* one body, not because of what we have done, but because of what God has done in Jesus Christ. This is the miracle, the mystery, and the burden of the church: we are related by blood (not ours but Christ's) to people we, humanly speaking, might avoid like the plague.

This is the gospel. We who through sin are estranged from God and one another have been reconciled by a divine love so astonishing and unmerited that we call it grace. And this reconciling grace is not just declared by some oracle or prophet. It is embodied, made incarnate, in a rabbi from Nazareth, whose continued presence is visible — embodied — in and through the community of his followers, the church. Let me offer another oxymoron: "individual Christian." To be a Christian is to be incorporated into that community whose very existence should bear visible witness to our Lord.

And that's why our division veils the gospel. Yes, Christians in the U.S. have, generally speaking, learned "to get along." But the current state of the church still says to the world that we have *not* found in Christ a center capable of holding us together; it says that the fragmentation of the world into bickering ideologies and like-minded enclaves is stronger than the reconciling power of God. The Mennonite theologian John Howard Yoder puts it very plainly: "Where Christians are not united, the gospel is not true in that place."[1]

Why care about Christian unity when there is so much other stuff to worry about? Because nothing less than the credibility of our faith is at stake!

I am afraid, however, that the church has been so co-opted by the culture that most Christians don't regard "divided church" as an oxymoron. Division is acceptable, taken for granted as an expression of our consumerist society. Some people like Pepsi, some like Coke; some are Catholics, some are Presbyterians. . . . We may not like to admit it, but the relationship among American denominations is basically predatory, like that of corporations. We cooperate when it is expedient to do so, but congregations, in effect, compete for each other's members in an anxious battle for market share — since size is often taken as the ultimate measure of success. If visitors come from the church down the street, few pastors or lay leaders will have qualms about recruiting them for "our team."

My intent in this final chapter is not to point fingers (I have done my share of recruiting), but rather to record how far we are from New Testament Christianity. In the early days of the church, baptized persons traveling to another city would carry a letter from their bishop so they could receive the eucharist in that city's congregation. "The bishop's or the pastor's job," writes Lutheran scholar Bruce Marshall, "was not to steal someone else's sheep, but to shepherd any member of the one flock who [happened] to come within . . . reach." There was certainly conflict in the early church (just read the letters to the Corinthians), but the idea of competing for members would have been incomprehensible. As Marshall puts it, "You don't prey upon your own body."[2]

In order to underscore why all of this matters, let me use another example

---

1. John Howard Yoder, *The Royal Priesthood* (Grand Rapids: Eerdmans, 1994), p. 291.
2. Bruce D. Marshall, "Who Really Cares About Christian Unity?" *First Things* 109 (January 2000): 29-34.

from the Amish. Many readers will recall that in 2006 ten Amish children were shot, five of them fatally, near Nickel Mines, Pennsylvania. All of us lament this awful tragedy. And we also likely remember how the Amish community responded — with extraordinary acts of forgiveness, comforting the killer's widow and establishing a fund for his family. They weren't being "nice"; they were giving expression to who they are as followers of Christ. They embodied the gospel, giving more effective witness than ten thousand sermons.

This is the key insight of what we call the ecumenical movement: Christians bear witness to reconciling grace not just by what we say or by what we do (though important!), but by what we are — by the way we live with one another. Friedrich Nietzsche once said that he might believe in their Redeemer if only Christ's followers would look more redeemed! Or let's put it in scriptural terms: "By this everyone will know that you are my disciples, if you have love for one another" (John 13:35).

I write these words on the eve of Advent, during which we will proclaim the coming of the "Prince of Peace." But the credibility of this awesome message will again be undercut by the incredible fragmentation of the messengers. Paul spends more time telling new Christians in Corinth and Rome how to live with one another than he does admonishing them to spread the Good News. Why? Because life in this new kind of community — Jew and Gentile, black and white, rich and poor, Chinese and American, liberal and conservative, Catholic and Protestant — is central to the gospel we proclaim.

The focus of the ecumenical movement is the church, its unity and renewal, but it is important to get the sequence right. According to Scripture, "God so loved the *world*" (John 3:16). The church is *not* the *ultimate* focus of God's concern; it is to be an appetizer of the promised banquet, a demonstration project of God's promised reign. Our unity as followers of Christ should be a prophetic challenge to those who seek to carve up the world for their own purposes and benefit. Our unity in Christ should be a prophetic challenge to economic structures that split the world into obscenely rich and abysmally poor, relegating billions of God's children to grinding poverty. Our unity in Christ should be a prophetic challenge to systems that dehumanize military or political opponents and value national boundaries over human solidarity.

Councils of churches often advocate on behalf of such things as health care and immigration reform, not (at least, at their best) because of their politics but because of their theology. We know that *every* neighbor deserves to be treated with dignity as one who bears God's image, and that welcoming the stranger is a reflection of our interconnectedness in God's one Creation. We are called to model this in the church for the sake of the world God so loves.

Why care about Christian unity when we have so much other stuff to worry about? Imagine if the churches in your place actually saw their life together as an intimate part of their own identity. What if they changed their grammar so that Methodist or Baptist or Catholic or Presbyterian became adjectives instead of nouns — Methodist *Christians* and Catholic *Christians* for whom shared life is far more than an add-on to their "real identity"? Imagine the witness we would make!

This doesn't mean, of course, that Christians agree on all things. Councils of churches and other ecumenical bodies should be spaces in which churches can explore their differences about issues that matter deeply — while remaining firmly in fellowship. Imagine what a witness *that* could make in a society that seems to equate community with ideological conformity.

I will end by returning to the Amish. I was born in Bloomfield, Iowa, home to a large Amish community, and later went to grade school in Kalona, Iowa, another center of Amish life. So I knew a few Amish kids, bought corn and strawberries from Amish farms. These are people I deeply respect.

I am afraid, however, that "ecumenical Amish" is yet another oxymoron. The Amish fear that ecumenical relations would water down their commitment to the truth of the gospel. I understand this position, but I also respectfully disagree. Our unity with one another is itself a central gospel truth. That's the point of the "body" metaphor. As the great missionary Lesslie Newbigin once put it, "A bagful of eyes is not a body."[3] Others should look at the churches that make up a council or other ecumenical gathering and say, "I wonder what holds *them* together. I wonder what *they* have in common" — which is when we point to Jesus Christ.

It is from those who are unlike ourselves that we may discover dimensions of the faith that we, on our own, would have overlooked. Without each other we are impoverished. But with each other we bear witness to a love that casts out fear (1 John 4:18) and frees us to live trustfully with difference.

At the heart of Paul's theology is this great verse from Romans 15 (quoted frequently in this book): "Welcome one another, therefore, just as Christ has welcomed you, for the glory of God" (v. 7). We have been welcomed by unconditional love, which we extend to one another as a sign of what God intends for all the world — that God may be glorified. This is the gospel! Thanks be to God!

---

3. Lesslie Newbigin, *The Gospel in a Pluralist Society* (Grand Rapids: Eerdmans, 1989), p. 231.

Index

United churches, 6, 155-56, 157
United Nations, 46, 105, 113, 122, 155
Unity, 38-40; and diversity, 39, 57; and eschatology, 44, 61-62; and justice, 56-65; why care about, 160-63
"Unity of the Church as Koinonia: Gift and Calling, The" [WCC], 34, 36-44

Vatican, Pontifical Council for Interreligious Dialogue, 99, 102
"Violence, Nonviolence, and the Struggle for Social Justice" [WCC], 25, 26, 28
Vischer, Lukas, 5, 158
Visser 't Hooft, Willem, 23, 63-64

Week of Prayer for Christian Unity, 81, 153
Wheeler, Barbara, 31-32

World Council of Churches (WCC), 4, 11, 22, 23, 25, 26, 34, 48, 58, 63, 66, 78-79, 92, 99, 101, 117, 155, 156, 157; assemblies of, Amsterdam (1949), 24, 31, 38, 137-38; Evanston (1954), 153; New Delhi (1961), 14, 37, 47, 96; Uppsala (1968), 156-57; Nairobi (1975), 26, 49, 62; Vancouver (1983), 26, 49, 58; Canberra (1991), 34; Porto Alegre (2006), 25, 34, 37, 38, 107, 158
World Evangelical Alliance (WEA), 99, 102

Yoder, John Howard, 161

Zizioulas, John (Metropolitan John of Pergamon), 51, 96, 97, 98